The Semiotics of Heritage Tourism

TOURISM AND CULTURAL CHANGE
Series Editors: Professor Mike Robinson, *Ironbridge International Institute for Cultural Heritage, University of Birmingham, UK* and Dr Alison Phipps, *University of Glasgow, Scotland, UK*

TCC is a series of books that explores the complex and ever-changing relationship between tourism and culture(s). The series focuses on the ways that places, peoples, pasts, and ways of life are increasingly shaped/transformed/created/packaged for touristic purposes. The series examines the ways tourism utilises/makes and re-makes cultural capital in its various guises (visual and performing arts, crafts, festivals, built heritage, cuisine, etc.) and the multifarious political, economic, social and ethical issues that are raised as a consequence.

Understanding tourism's relationships with culture(s) and vice versa, is of ever-increasing significance in a globalising world. This series will critically examine the dynamic inter-relationships between tourism and culture(s). Theoretical explorations, research-informed analyses, and detailed historical reviews from a variety of disciplinary perspectives are invited to consider such relationships.

Full details of all the books in this series and of all our other publications can be found on http://www.channelviewpublications.com, or by writing to Channel View Publications, St Nicholas House, 31–34 High Street, Bristol BS1 2AW, UK.

The Semiotics of Heritage Tourism

Emma Waterton and Steve Watson

CHANNEL VIEW PUBLICATIONS
Bristol • Buffalo • Toronto

Library of Congress Cataloging in Publication Data
Waterton, Emma.
The Semiotics of Heritage Tourism/Emma Waterton and Steve Watson.
Tourism and Cultural Change: 35
Includes bibliographical references and index.
1. Heritage tourism. 2. Culture—Semiotic models. I. Title.
G156.5.H47W37 2014
306.4'819014–dc23 2013034219

British Library Cataloguing in Publication Data
A catalogue entry for this book is available from the British Library.

ISBN-13: 978-1-84541-421-4 (hbk)
ISBN-13: 978-1-84541-420-7 (pbk)

Channel View Publications
UK: St Nicholas House, 31–34 High Street, Bristol BS1 2AW, UK.
USA: UTP, 2250 Military Road, Tonawanda, NY 14150, USA.
Canada: UTP, 5201 Dufferin Street, North York, Ontario M3H 5T8, Canada.

Copyright © 2014 Emma Waterton and Steve Watson.

All rights reserved. No part of this work may be reproduced in any form or by any means without permission in writing from the publisher.

The policy of Multilingual Matters/Channel View Publications is to use papers that are natural, renewable and recyclable products, made from wood grown in sustainable forests. In the manufacturing process of our books, and to further support our policy, preference is given to printers that have FSC and PEFC Chain of Custody certification. The FSC and/or PEFC logos will appear on those books where full certification has been granted to the printer concerned.

Typeset by Techset Composition India (P) Ltd., Bangalore and Chennai, India.
Printed and bound in Great Britain by Short Run Press Ltd.

Contents

	Acknowledgements	vii
1	An Introduction	1
	Expanding the Semiotic	3
	The Structure	8
2	Advancing Theory	11
	The Semiotic Landscape	11
	Signs of the Times: An Historical Overview	13
	Conclusion	31
3	Signing the Past	32
	Cultural Context and Cultural Process	33
	The Genealogies of Heritage Tourism	37
	Seeing is Believing: Heritage Attractions and Visuality	45
	Conclusion	50
4	Marketing the Past	53
	Discourse and the Marketing Narrative	54
	Semiotics and the Heritage 'Product'	57
	Heritage Tourism and Marketing Narratives	60
	The Organization of Marketing Narratives	63
	Being There	68
	Conclusion	73
5	Remembering	75
	A New Theory of Signification	75
	Embodied Remembering	77
	Remembering and Photography	85
	Conclusion	96

6 Living with the Past   98
   Semiotics in Place: Everyday Objects and Experiences   99
   The Feeling of Temporal Depth   103
   De-Differentiating Here and There   105
   Intensity and Indifference in Heritage Tourism   107
   Conclusion   115

7 Conclusions   117
   A New Semiotics of Heritage Tourism   118
   The Implications for Critical Studies in Heritage Tourism   120
   Some Final Words...   121

   References   124
   Index   137

Acknowledgements

Any book is a complex undertaking and something of a journey. We can just about remember where and how we started this, but we do remember clearly all the people that helped us along the way, especially when the direction seemed unclear or the pace began to flag a little. We acknowledge, with gratitude, the generous help and guidance of Sarah Williams, our commissioning editor at Channel View, whose patience in the latter stages was a source of much relief. Once we were underway our families, friends and colleagues provided that very special kind of encouragement and moral support that only comes from those who understand: Robyn Bushell and Russell Staiff at the University of Western Sydney, Glyn Littlewood at York St John University and Rosa Gonzalez at the University of Seville. Our particular thanks go to Christine Mortimer at York St John for wrestling so heroically with the first draft and to Duncan Light who, with patience and immense generosity with his time, effort and scholarship, gently questioned and challenged our often uncertain thoughts. To all of them a monumental thank you and we hope the book repays their support. Its shortcomings, however, are ours and ours alone.

1 An Introduction

As researchers interested in heritage we are no strangers to travel. Indeed, we have had the good fortune of visiting quite a number of heritage tourism sites, both the iconic and those less so. To some we arrived already prepared and informed, well-thumbed guidebooks clutched in our hands and firm plans drafted to capture the multiple experiences we have heard about elsewhere. At others, we shuffled onto the scene far less certain, with only the slightest inkling of what we might encounter and feeling in those moments a nervousness – fear almost – of the unknown. There have been, too, occasions that have erupted as curious mixtures of the two, in which our informed expectations were exceeded or disrupted by atmospheres that modulate our behaviour in ways we could never have anticipated. Visiting the city of Derry in Northern Ireland is a good case in point, for this is a city with a serious reputation. Even if one were to turn up there without the tourist's requisite and dog-eared copy of the *Lonely Planet Guide*, there is a chance its reputation would precede it, if only through the U2 song, 'Sunday Bloody Sunday', released in 1983. We might know, for example, something about 'The Troubles'; perhaps, too, we may recollect something about the Apprentice Boys or the 'Battle of Bogside'. Certainly, we might expect to see depictions of the city's history etched onto its everyday landscape, with urban murals spatially articulating a reminder of the politics, violence and bloodshed. We could easily anticipate such physical traces and historical disclosures, and in so doing encounter a city that looks very much how we always imagined it to be.

But our bodies are never really detached from what we are visiting: our skin, ears, nose, fingertips, feet, stomach and heart register things, too. Yet sometimes this capacity for a place like Derry to *affect*, to get inside us bodily, can come as a surprise. While we anticipate the history, we may be less expecting of the sense of haunting that accompanies difficult pasts. We may never, until that moment, have paused to really consider the way traumatic memories can hang in the air or colour a space, shadowing landscapes in ways that toy with our own moods. We might not previously have thought about how such moods, and the moods of others, are contagious, stirring up feelings of anxiety and discomfort, relentlessly. Perhaps the sky is overcast on the day of a visit, provoking only muted conversation and a solemnity that works to further intensify the moment. Nonetheless, standing among the city's buildings, in the midst of its streetscapes, surfaces and a medley of murals, we often find ourselves opening up to an atmosphere that is charged with emotion that links us directly with the history and politics of the place: dissonance, conflict, violence and the potentialities of a new found peace. Here, again, it begs an understanding of the ways in which these meanings and impressions are vectored towards us, around us and between us.

This concern with atmosphere and emotion dislodges something that has become established in the semiotic canon – and that is the dominance of 'the visual' and its concern with ways of seeing the world. That said, it is hardly surprising that the visual, to date, has remained the dominant sense in this and many other contexts. It is implicated in the long development of western culture with its obsessive interest in text, image and the iconic. The milestone moment of the introduction of perspective and the re-introduction of classical realism into the visual arts in the 15th century still reverberates. Likewise, the introduction of printing and the mechanical reproduction of text and images continues today on a scale unimaginable just a few decades ago, thanks to the inherent visualities of cyberspace. Our understanding of heritage tourism is naturally influenced by these visualities, as indeed is the practice of tourism itself, as discussed in its discursive contexts by Jaworski and Pritchard (2005), with its central practice of 'sight-seeing', its strange rituals of photography and the anticipations that energize the tourist gaze. But it has long been understood that other senses are implicated in tourist practice, and that the presence of the body itself is an essential prerequisite, even though this has been largely overlooked when what is seen is so often *all* that is seen (Crouch, 2000, 2011; also Robinson, 2012; Waade & Jørgensen, 2010).

This provides our point of departure, the potential to contribute to a changing perspective. While this is a book that explores the semiotics of heritage tourism, it will be obvious from our opening paragraphs that it does so in a way that seeks to dislodge the dominance of 'the visual' from this type of theorizing and more fully explore the complexity involved in meaning- and sense-making processes within heritage tourism, especially where this is now such a globalized phenomenon replete with a variety of experiences and cultural productions, all of which demand more complex and sophisticated forms of analysis (Jaworski & Pritchard, 2005: 5–7). Of course, we remain interested in the iconic, the intense and all those sites and experiences that seem so neatly and easily to gather together the visual and the emotional.

But we are interested, too, in those quieter, often more banal, places. Because in them there can gather an intensity that flickers, just for us: a memory triggered from childhood; the chance to finally unwind and relax; to be with friends, family or alone. But if this is to be our point of departure, we need to be clear about what we are taking with us and what we are leaving behind. Critiques of the visual have emerged in the broader social sciences as well as those disciplines and fields more closely related to heritage, such as archaeology, anthropology, cultural studies and tourism. While it no longer seems supportable to 'privilege' the visual in quite the way it always has been, it is still hugely significant. Indeed, informed by a range of broader philosophical developments, such as post-structuralism and postmodernism, it is a concept that has been revivified time and again, in concepts such as 'representation', 'signification', 'visuality' and so forth. As Castree and MacMillan (2004: 471) have so powerfully argued, '[t]here is more to the world than representation...but representation is nonetheless a powerful world-disclosing and world-changing technology. That is, it is practical and performative; it is a tool and it assuredly has effects'.

And so, with all this in mind, the explorations of heritage found in this book take the visual and its representational corollaries forward, but combine them with other elements associated with non- or more-than-representational theory. Broader notions of performativity and experience that are well established in the literature, and especially in this series (see for example Lee Jolliffe's explorations of the intersections of global products, such as tea (2007), coffee (2010) and sugar (2012), with cultural production and heritage; see also Jack & Phipps, 2005), provide the backdrop. In acknowledging the broader frameworks of analysis that such studies imply, we are interested in the particular aspects of emotion and affect that can be sensed in the landscapes of heritage tourism and the way that these, as embodied experiences, can interact with the representational aspects of those same landscapes. That sets out our stall, but there is a trajectory of thinking and theoretical development that is in itself relevant to the way this book unfolds, and which forms the core of the following chapter. First, however, we lay out our broader theoretical intentions.

Expanding the Semiotic

Both tourism and heritage are fields that are well established as being inherently visual, with the ubiquity of maps, brochures, paintings, websites, landscapes, advertisements and movies all 'speaking' to the centrality of the image. This multimodal textuality as a characteristic of tourism discourse has been noted previously and applied in case studies and research (see especially Jaworski & Pritchard, 2005, for an important contribution in this series). Indeed, there is considerable scholarship around these topics, with almost every scholar in the field finding some level of familiarity with early studies on postcards, brochures and photographs, whether it be that penned by Chalfen (1979), Albers and James (1988) or Mellinger (1994), perhaps. More profoundly still, we expect that it would be the work of Dean MacCannell (1976) on *The Tourist* and John Urry's work on *The Tourist Gaze* (1990) that springs to mind for most as paving the way for a 'visual turn' within both fields (see Palmer, 2009: 75; Waterton & Watson, 2010). While this literature is undoubtedly an established and critical part of the academic canon, it is now being asked to respond to and accommodate more recent developments in theory that are focused on immediacy and engagement rather than the more familiar post-structuralist accounts of symbolic and ideological representation (see Jack & Phipps, 2005; Picard & Robinson, 2012). This sort of emergent theory, which focuses upon emotion, performance, embodiment and experience, poses a challenge to the ways in which 'the semiotic' is seen to work in the formation of heritage tourism meanings, from both an empirical and theoretical standpoint (see work by Little, 2010; Waade & Jørgensen, 2010, as examples).

Moving in this direction, it is important to be clear about the way that performativity and experience articulate with the symbolic realm and what the implications are for expanding the semiotic. To start with, we want to be explicit about how much of the canon of non-representational theory (often referred to with the shorthand NRT, though we prefer the phrase suggested by Hayden Lorimer (2005) 'more-than-representational') will be touched upon in this volume. While clearly informed and influenced by this broader theoretical agenda, we offer more of a flirtation, to borrow from Crouch (2010b), as we are content to leave its harder theorizations aside for this volume (but see Waterton & Watson, 2013). Instead, the key issue that we will press forward with is affect, including its politics, affordances, registers and emotional formulations. The reason for this, as intimated above, draws from an acknowledgement of the significance of 'the body' in tourism and its role in registering, experiencing and responding to touristic places. Like others before us (see Veijola & Jokinen, 1994), we are drawn to the argument that it is the body that is responsible for framing touristic experiences and that it does this in a variety of ways: from the desire and anticipation that influences behaviour (Pritchard & Morgan, 2010), motivation and choice, to movement, through travel itineraries, touring, wandering, gazing, exploring, visiting attractions, eating, feeling tired, feeling sick, waiting in airports and railway stations, walking down a street, feeling light and shade, happiness, gloom, boredom, excitement and disappointment. Indeed, there is a whole repertoire of embodied performances and sense registers rooted in the framing of tourist experiences that hinge upon the body. Seen from this angle, representations are not only contextualized, they seem like the icing on the cake. But they are not, as Robinson (2012: 41) has stated:

> While it is no doubt the case that the sights, sounds, tastes, smells and touch of the world can stimulate our emotions what we feel, how we feel it and importantly, how we comprehend and express what we feel, is far more complex. As tourists we have moments of joy, moments of sadness, anger and fear (and much angst), often fleeting, often within close proximity of each other; emotions that we would not have experienced had we not travelled. But we also bring our emotions to bear upon the world; our histories and understandings of encounter.

So emotions, affects and representations of these are closely interwoven, and never more so than in that culminating act of framing in tourism – the taking of a photograph. Here, the body is posed and poised, both as photographer and photographed, and represented *in situ* in relation to other bodies, spaces, places and predispositions that emerge from representations and existing narratives.

For heritage tourists, the photograph is the culmination of the sight/site as seen (and for this reason often replicates established viewpoints depicted in guidebooks, brochures and postcards), but it also affords opportunities to capture moments of engagement with heritage objects by framing them in certain ways or by putting ourselves in the picture, juxtaposed, expressively, in relation to the objects and places concerned. For us, then, the photograph is emblematic of the embodied nature of the tourist experience and is affective to the extent that it is produced in moments of engagement that are less than expressive and at the same time more than representational, which is an idea we develop from the work of Bærenholdt *et al.* (2004). Our engagement with photography itself is, of course, nothing new. Indeed, the coalescence of heritage, tourism and photography is reflective of a far longer history, tracing back at least to the Renaissance and, particularly, its concerns with the scopic qualities of modern travel. These, Osborne (2000: 4) argues, prompted a need to 'explore in every direction', in order to:

> ... fill a great emptiness that had opened up in the cosmology and the sense of self of many Europeans ... this emptiness induced the urge to travel, to fill the spatial void with human presence, or to find whatever was imagined to have been lost. It impelled the creation of images to fill

the vacant spaces with human features and meanings or to draw the dreamer or traveller towards a world that might be repossessed.

Unsurprisingly, the urging underpinning of early photography combined easily with European imperial expansion in the 19th century, with the two working in tandem to extend the reach of western scopicity. As Osborne (2000: 7–8) goes on to argue, this bringing together of visual representation, travel and the colonial enterprise introduced an interest in visual–observational approaches as a mechanism that allowed an escape from the limitations of traditional modes of description. The role of heritage objects in this visual nexus is also historically formulated, not least because historical objects, such as those of the Grand Tour, the Arcadian, the picturesque and the romantic, have become so deeply embedded in the experience of heritage tourism. As Osborne (2000: 82) implies, though he is focusing specifically on what he sees as the allure of ruins as '[e]mblems of lost times', such historical objects, heritage places and associated experiences:

...have long featured in tourism's itineraries expressing, as Dean MacCannell has demonstrated, modern society's desire to recover, in the cultures of other places and other epochs, the authenticity it imagines it has lost in its own.

The relationship between heritage and tourism, and the link they collectively share with photography, thus creates a dual concern with the visual and what it might mean in a culturally modulated sign system, such that:

[t]he effects of photography's presence in the tourist system merely complete[s] a process under way before photography's birth. (Osborne, 2000: 82)

While we do not want to go into historical territory already explored, suffice it to say that it is hardly surprising that semiotics, as it has been conventionally construed, has nestled in the visual whenever it has ventured from the textual and, indeed, that the visual has been its first port of call when text has been exhausted. But the body in tourism opens up further avenues of semiotic analysis. The way the body is, feels and moves in space generates meanings of its own that stand in relation to the visual and the representational. An example of this occurred to us when we were completing this book in Los Angeles. Our visit there inevitably included time out for a trip to Hollywood, where a conventional symbol, the famous and iconic 'Hollywood' sign on the hillside overlooking Hollywood Boulevard and the

Sunset Strip (see Figure 1.1), might be expected to energize our engagement with the place. It did not.

Instead, our tiredness after a busy day, our need to rush to make it to a theatre performance and our protracted wait in the queue outside the theatre constituted an embodied, experiential intervention that disrupted the power of the sign. Our tiredness and irritation left us deflated and underwhelmed. The Hollywood sign seemed small and insignificant, and Hollywood itself felt scruffy, tired and dismissive. The active semiotic, in both the name 'Hollywood' and the sign itself, seemed to refer to something in the imagination rather than anything we were experiencing directly by being there.

This relationship between bodies, experience and representation is central to the lines of enquiry posited in this book and the way that we employ affect to open the debate. By focusing on broader notions of engagement, the volume holds at its core the intention of developing a richer understanding of heritage tourism, one that takes account of more recent thinking, in both visuality and performativity, in an attempt to grasp the sensual, emotive and embodied aspects of heritage tourist experiences. The book therefore adopts an approach that both briefly reviews the traditional role of semiotics in heritage tourism *as well as* proposing an agenda for future research, an agenda that has been made more pressing by the emergence of, and challenges posed by, more-than-representational theory and its associated concepts of

Figure 1.1 The Hollywood sign (*Source:* Emma Waterton)

emergent meaning and performativity. This theoretical advance re-evaluates the significance of semiotic analysis in heritage tourism at a time when there are major developments taking place in the theoretical landscape that surrounds it. Key to this will be a thorough exploration of the role of semiotic analysis within this emerging theoretical landscape, identifying not only valid and viable methods of analysis, but the forms emerging research might take.

The Structure

The volume opens with a historicizing of semiotic theory and reflections on its relevance to heritage tourism in a chapter we have called *Advancing Theory*. To commence the piecing together of our own particular theoretical framing, the chapter begins with a review of broader semiotic interventions, focusing particularly (and unsurprisingly) on the pioneering work of Ferdinand de Saussure and Charles Peirce, before turning to examine the semiotic inquiries that have been undertaken in the fields of tourism and heritage studies more specifically. There, the work of key authors, including Dean MacCannell, John Urry, Annette Pritchard, Nigel Morgan and Catherine Palmer, among others, is foregrounded, particularly their post-structuralist inspired explorations of the symbolic workings of power and ideology within tourism representations. *Advancing Theory*, as the title suggests, also contains an articulation of what we have termed 'the semiotic landscape' of heritage tourism, which we see as broadening significantly the parameters of semiotic analysis in response to recent non- and more-than-representational theorizations. With this added dimension – the immediacy of experience – our theorizing of the semiotic landscape is moved to include the ways in which people encounter it, sensually, through corporeal proximity. The chapter therefore closes with a conceptualization of our immediate and experiential encounters with the affective atmospheres of heritage tourism sites and their semiotic landscapes.

The following chapter, *Signing the Past*, delves into an exploration of the deeper shared understandings of heritage and how this shapes tourism, along with the range of personal, local, regional and national identities it underpins. Given our overall intentions in this volume, the chapter foregrounds the ways in which the visual, specifically, is implicated in the semiotics of heritage tourism. To do so, it borrows its critical underpinning from what Laurajane Smith (2006) has labelled the 'Authorized Heritage Discourse', which we see as underpinning a range of dominant representations that are reproduced and reinforced within the heritage tourism sphere, representations that not only affect 'ways of seeing', but 'ways of doing' too. In particular, the chapter examines the powers of media producers involved in the creation and dissemination of meaning associated with heritage tourism attractions, foregrounding specifically the ways in which these players negotiate cultural meaning between competing audiences. The context for this examination is the conceptualization of social and cultural narratives, the social 'imaginary' of heritage and the engagement of individuals with these *a priori* constructs through the media and experiences of heritage tourism.

Our fourth chapter, *Marketing the Past*, contextualizes and theorizes the operational modalities of heritage tourism and its sustaining narratives. It begins with a closer inspection of the role played by discourse within the sphere of heritage tourism, before turning to examine a variety of textual and visual sources drawn upon and presented in the commodified world of heritage tourism. Extending from Chapter 3, this analysis loosely unfolds around post-structuralist and more-than-representational framings, beginning with an assessment of the ways in which designers, interpretation and services marketers construct the visual and symbolic experiences of heritage tourism, before attempting to unpack how these discursive techniques are used to potentially manipulate the subjective and affective responses of tourists. In extending our analysis beyond the symbolic and ideological constructions of the semiotic landscape, the chapter therefore necessarily engages with the significance of performativity in the context of engagement *in situ*. The chapter thus unfolds around a discussion of product development and its visuality within the context of sustaining narratives, followed by an exploration of the semiotics of selling the past. It concludes with reflections upon how visitors engage with, experience and are affected by the authorizing discourses peddled within the marketing of the past.

In the first of two chapters that attempt to tackle more concretely the affective atmospheres of the semiotic landscape, our fifth chapter, *Remembering*, turns to examine the cumulative, and historic, processes that mediate our engagements with heritage tourism sites. Key to this exploration is the notion of 'encounter', which draws attention to the dialogical processes through which visitors are drawn into inter-subjective and affective moments of engagement with heritage tourism sites, which, we argue, is a central locus for understanding the relationship between representational and non-representational perspectives. As such, this chapter conceptually allows for the energies, realities and responses of actual bodies as they move around and interpret the sites and experiences before them, caught up as they are in moments of affective contagion. Moreover, we argue that our ability to respond to such semiotic landscapes is in large part formed in processes of remembering – through our attempts to reconcile previous experiences, moments, knowledges and events. Indeed, it is precisely through these acts of bodily remembering that our engagements with heritage exceed their representations, with memories being remembered in moments of engagement, re-energized in our bodies where they are expressed once again and come to affect ourselves, other bodies and other representations.

In the second of our two substantive chapters exploring the more-than-representational, Chapter Six, *Living with the Past*, explores new sources of meaning for tourists in the form of their encounters with the everyday life of places. Here, the tangibilities, intangibilities and self-made experiences of visited spaces are separated from the authorized discourses that constitute them in the sphere of tourism, and there they are recast as personal and shared moments of engagement and meaning. Furthermore, it suggests (after Larsen, 2008b) a 'de-exoticising' of the touristic places, one that breaks down the representational aspects of heritage tourism *in situ* and redefines it in terms of subjective experience and contours of intensity that are expressive of both individual and collective meanings. The semiotic landscape is thus reconstituted as a space where representations interact with experience and engagement, and where affect and emotion are mobilized by and, in turn, mobilize representational practices.

Finally, *Conclusions* draws together the main themes of the book, and reflects on where the semiotic landscape in heritage tourism might be taken next, particularly in light of emerging theories of performativity within more-than-representational theory. Our conclusion is also a call to action for further research in heritage tourism and a mode of address that acknowledges the expanded semiotics offered by the body and all its senses in places and spaces that are, sometimes and for some people, a way of doing and feeling heritage tourism.

2 Advancing Theory

The Semiotic Landscape

The aim of this chapter is to examine the relevance of 'semiotics' to heritage tourism – a field that is both materially and visually framed. It begins from the premise that 'semiotics' is comprised of a suite of theoretical perspectives, each of which comes with an attendant set of analytical tools. In order to perform as the theoretical cog around which the rest of the volume turns, the chapter necessarily begins with a review of these past and prevailing theoretical approaches, before mapping out a potential future that draws inspiration from more recent sources. As with all histories of theory, such an examination is a large undertaking; too large, we could argue, especially as it carries with it the implicit promise of a journey that traverses multiple timeframes. This is because semiotic theories, in one guise or another, have been informing the field of heritage tourism for quite some time – we need only look to Dean MacCannell's *The Tourist* (1976) or John Urry's *The Tourist Gaze* (1990) to shore up our point. These are theories that have been asked to weather the passing of a good many '-isms', '-ologies' and 'turns', to borrow from Castree and MacMillan (2004), so much so that the net result is a vast theoretical terrain we can only hope to nod towards here. Nonetheless, it is an examination we see as important. Indeed, these reflections, while serving primarily to historicize semiotic theories within our own particular context, will also allow the chapter to carry out a broader purpose: that of signaling our intention to move thinking *about* heritage tourism, towards that which occurs *within* it (after Keane, 2003).

In order for this to happen, we first need to argue for a theoretical project that extends the semiotic focus of signs, symbols and sign-systems towards one that references a fuller, and more complex, corporeal performance. We thus begin our project of *Advancing Theory* with an attempt to adumbrate what we see as the two most historically relevant senses of 'semiotic theory': those underpinned by structuralist and post-structuralist thinking. Often coupled with talk of 'representation' and 'visuality', these approaches have been the most dominant within heritage tourism over the past three decades, especially so within a field that has tended towards the atheoretical for quite some time. While they will be explored within the context of those texts dealing specifically with heritage and/or tourism, such as those penned by Graburn (1989), MacCannell (1976) and Urry (1990), it should come as no surprise that the chapter also courts a broader range of philosophical thinkers, including Ferdinand de Saussure, Charles Sanders Peirce and Michel Foucault. These are thinkers who have helped capture the power of semiotics in some way, especially through their defining of terms like 'semiology' and 'discourse'. Perhaps most significantly however, they have done this by challenging us to rethink the idea that discourses and representations depict a pregiven world, and forcing us to collapse those essentialist notions that suppose that meaning is, or can be, fixed (Cox, 2011).

But the chapter is based on more than this. And like many others before us, we use the word 'more' here deliberately (see Lorimer, 2005; Roberts, 2012). This is because our aim is *not* to make a case for going beyond or against established semiotic theories; rather, we seek to *continue* with, or *renew*, critical semiotics with the aim of adding an engagement with the multisensual, experiential, embodied and performative. This is based on our belief that engagements with heritage – as tourists, users, people – are often resistant to analyses drawn up solely around theories of representation, and in any case, conventional representational theories only take us so far along this extended route. For us, then, theoretical discussions need to take up an edge that focuses not only on what a heritage place, interpretation or experience *seems* to mean or project, but what it *does* (after Cox, 2011). We thus find ourselves positioned very much within the cut-and-thrust of the theoretical context opened up primarily by Nigel Thrift and the newer 'non-representational' theories (Thrift, 2008). At face-value, his is a concern with what Jacobs and Nash (2003: 272) have described as the 'jaded and sterile focus on representation'. By way of solution, Thrift proposes that we turn towards the everyday, relational and affective, thus broadening our explorations of signs and discourse in an attempt to access, in some way, the prediscursive and precognitive (Thrift, 2008; Jacobs & Nash, 2003). While this may read as an attempt to supersede an established philosophical position, we are assuredly *not* advocating a theoretical turn that is *anti*-representational. Neither, for that matter, is Thrift. Indeed, we are in no way agnostic about the critical work undertaken by those concerned with representation. More accurately, to borrow from Castree and MacMillan (2004: 470), our aim is to argue for a theoretical project that includes a return of the old, '... the finessing of important insights, themes, concepts, techniques, or what have you, in the belief that they still offer ... something of value in the present'. Striking that balance – and, moreover, convincing our readers that we have done so – is the central challenge of this chapter.

Signs of the Times: An Historical Overview

Representations, communication, gestures, signs, images, symbols, language – this is what makes us human. In order to collect these terms together, we have borrowed the phrase 'the semiotic landscape' from Kress and van Leeuwen (2006). We use that phrase to 'speak' about the overarching scope of the book, as it is one we feel enables us to gesture towards our intentions of incorporating a fuller range of communicative modes of signification and meaning within our analysis of heritage tourism. That said, the tourism industry, and heritage tourism more specifically, remains a field that is inherently visual, awash with images and representations (see Waterton & Watson, 2010). This is something we remain mindful of throughout the chapter and volume. No clearer demonstration of this centrality is needed than the term 'sight-seeing', which brings with it ubiquitous visions of ambling tourists, equipped with some form of camera or camera-enabled mobile device. The vast array of maps, brochures, paintings, websites, landscapes, advertisements, movies and such that are associated with heritage tourism likewise attest to the staying power of the visual as *the* mode of communication within the field. In this mix, it has often been the photograph that has held our attention most avidly. Indeed, since the Kodak revolution of the 1880s, followed by the increasing popularity of the picture postcard in the 1900s, tourism has been 'unimaginable without photography', as Osborne (2000: 20) points out. It is this lingering association that has prompted us to continue with a focus on photography in this volume. In this, we are interested in the very presence of a photograph*ing* body, which has more recently come into focus and reminded us that there is something more at play here, something we should think about in addition to the representational worlds of photographs themselves – its theatrics, subjectivity and embodied nature (Larsen, 2008a: 143; see also Chapter 5).

For us, then, the camera – its use(r)s, the process of photographing, the resultant photos – seems to serve as a kind of 'sign of the times' for the trajectories we explore in this section, simplified though they inevitably are here. We could have picked any number of practices associated with heritage tourism, but given the limits of the volume we have chosen to focus most specifically upon this particular facet of the heritage tourism experience.

In doing so, for example, we can begin our theoretical account with reflections on structuralism, which tends to revolve around questions to do with what and how a representation *means*. This underpinning loosely speaks to those assumptions that a camera could be objective in nature, truthful and unbiased. Its photographs, by extension, were taken to be scientific, unproblematically reflecting *the* world and thereby confirming a 'representation–reality' dualism (Roberts, 2012; see also Sturken & Cartwright, 2009). Next, we consider the more dominant outpourings of post-structural thinking revolving around 'discourse', which can also be exposed in emerging concerns that the camera could be deceptive in character, coding and producing particular ways of seeing. Its photographs, by extension, ruptured the dualism and forced us to think through social contexts and relations of power in order to grasp the ideological practices that sit behind them (Roberts, 2012). Finally, we turn to non- or more-than-representational accounts, also post-structuralist in nature, though until now more muted, which position the camera, along with its attendant processes of photograph*ing*, as something that is always in the making, emergent and informing. Its photographs force us to consider the camera and its user, the process, as caught up in performances in which places, objects and people are toured and remade.

What should have become obvious from our reflections so far is that our semiotic landscape extends far beyond the purview of visuality alone. In it, we see texts, images, dress, movements, narratives, architecture, gestures, practices, artworks, music, video and so on. The important point is that whichever genre of (non-)representation we metaphorically pick up to examine, it will inevitably share in the fact that each text, gesture and so forth is always imbued with power and politics. In addition, as powerful forms of communication, they also always operate along the lines of particular social relations and bring with them the capacity to 'move' and 'shift' intertextually, cohering 'internally with each other and externally with the context in and for which they were produced' (Kress & van Leeuwen, 2006: 43). The semiotics of heritage tourism is thus always a reiterative process of production, circulation and consumption: along the way, particular renditions of sites, tourists and experiences achieve naturalization, yet, as we will argue in much of the remainder of this book, those representations are simultaneously open to processes of destabilization through performative processes of engagement and contestation (after Butler, 1993). Already, the influences of structuralist and post-structuralist (including non-representational) thinking are observable in our summations of the semiotic landscape; that said, it would probably be fair to say that we have doubts about the theoretical utility of each if used on their own. What follows, then, is a condensing of the salient elements of all three approaches, before we move on to piece together our own semiotic landscape.

Signs of the times: The structuralist influence

Generally understood to mean 'the study of signs and sign systems as modes of communication', semiotics has been a dominant and recurring theme in heritage tourism and tourism studies for some time (Foote & Azaryahu, 2009: 89; see also Echtner, 1999). Those scholars taking up a semiotic agenda will, more often than not, turn to a style of structuralist thinking associated with Ferdinand de Saussure – a Swiss linguist – and Charles Sanders Peirce – an American philosopher and logician – to help historicize their understandings of the mechanisms of meaning, or, in our case, how people encode and decode the touristic spaces they encounter and experience (see Echtner, 1999; Metro-Roland, 2009; Pennington & Thomsen, 2010). For example, when Morgan and Pritchard (1998) wrote of the tourist as semiotician, they were drawing not only on Culler's (1990) well-cited essay on the subject, as well as Urry's work on 'the gaze', they were also reflecting particular renderings of structuralist theory in which arbitrary connections, cultural in nature, are assumed to form around particular objects or places and an associated suite of meanings:

> One learns that a thatched cottage with roses around the door represents 'ye olde England', or the waves crushing on to rocks signifies 'wild, untamed nature'; or especially, that a person with a camera draped around his/her neck is clearly a tourist. (Morgan & Pritchard, 1998: 33)

Given the ubiquity of these sorts of suppositions, structuralist-inspired semiotics, which commence with attempts to document *how* the 'clear "rules" – or structures – which govern the formation of all communication' can be used to translate representations into meaning, seems to us to be a logical place to start (Hall, 1997: 6; Webb, 2009: 45). The work of Ferdinand de Saussure is particularly informative here, as it is he, more than anyone, who is credited with many of the terms (sign, signifier, signified, etc.) fundamental to the practice of 'semiology', which he defined as the 'science that studies signs within society' (de Saussure, 1916: 16, cited in Echtner, 1999: 48). His semiotic approach was very much informed by constructivist thinking and is based on the acknowledgement that language is social in nature (Hall, 1997). This, in itself, signalled a strong break with earlier assumptions built up around a belief in the mimetic or reflective character of representation, or the perceived transparency between words and things (Hall, 1997: 35). Key to his thinking is the concept of the 'sign', which, for de Saussure, is comprised of a signifier (image, word or sound pattern) and a signified (meaning or concept with which the signifier is associated) (Radford & Radford, 2005). A signifier exists as the entity that represents, with the sign operating as a combination of that signifier and what it *means* (Sturken & Cartwright, 2009). In heritage tourism terms, the sign would equate to any given heritage site, for example the USS Arizona Memorial (Figure 2.1), which is marked out with signage, brochures, postcards and so forth (signifiers) as a commemorative tourist sight (signified). Any cursory flick through early tourism texts dealing with imagery or representation will offer a good indication of his influence, as there can be found scholars such as Urry (1990) and Selwyn (1996), among others, reflecting his thinking.

In essence, de Saussure (1915 [1966]: 113) argued that '... language is a system in which all elements fit together, and in which the value of any one element depends on the simultaneous coexistence of all the others'. Yet while 'language' is foregrounded, with sounds, written words and images earmarked as those things capable of functioning as signs *within language*, it is important to note that a range of material objects can operate in that capacity too (Hall, 1997). What is significant about de Saussure's semiotic theory is his conceptualization of those relationships between each element as arbitrary. Here, we are introduced to the centrality of difference, which is mapped

Figure 2.1 The USS Arizona Memorial (*Source:* Emma Waterton)

out within a static system and most usefully evidenced by means of internal binary oppositions. Crucially, then, it is patterns, operating at the heart of what is envisioned as a closed system and built around familiar binaries, such as self/other, home/away, authentic/inauthentic, everyday/extraordinary and sacred/profane, that form the basis for much of de Saussure's structuralist-inspired analysis, which later infused the structural anthropology of Lévi-Strauss (1963) and his concerns with myth, kinship and totemism.

In addition to his two-part model of the sign, which aligns the 'signified' with the 'signifier', de Saussure's influence can also be seen in the lingering distinctions implied between ideas and things, the sign and the world, or the linguistic system and 'actual instances of discourse' or its materializations (Keane, 2003: 42). Given the arbitrary relationship between signifiers and signifieds, historical influence comes to play a key role in de Saussure's imaginings. As Culler points out:

> Because it is arbitrary, the sign is totally subject to history and the combination at the particular moment of a given signifier and signified is a contingent result of the historical process. (Culler, 1976: 36)

This understanding continues to play a significant role in debates about the meaning of heritage in contemporary society, a point which will be revisited in greater depth in Chapter 3.

Like de Saussure, Charles Sanders Peirce's work has been profoundly influential for our understandings of semiology. Peirce's work similarly developed out of a working of the relationship between a 'signifier' and that which is 'signified', but to that he added the distinction of a third category, the 'interpretant', which posits that the overarching 'sign' must also '... *stand for something to somebody* in a certain respect' (Echtner, 1999: 48 (original emphasis); Kress & van Leeuwen, 2006: 8). His resultant semiotic triad, which is recursive, hybrid and processual in nature, thus moves from and between the 'designatum' (or object/concept – real or imagined), the 'sign' (or signifier) and the 'interpretant' (the resulting action/thought, or, in other words, the one interpreting the sign and their collateral experiences), all three of which are essential within Peirce's framework (Echtner, 1999: 48; Pennington & Thomsen, 2010). Though de Saussure clearly conceived of a passage of meaning, it is Peirce who offers the most explicit understanding of this process. He sums up the relationships between the three concepts in the following way, beginning from the notion that the sign is:

> ...something which stands to somebody for something in some respect or capacity. It addresses somebody, that is, creates in the mind of that

person an equivalent sign, or perhaps a more developed sign ... The sign stands for something, its object. It stands for that *object*, not in all respects, but in reference to a sort of idea. (Peirce, 1955: 99; cited in Webb, 2009: 46 (original emphasis))

The designatum is understood as being either 'immediate' or 'dynamical', and the interpretant is split between the 'immediate', 'dynamical' and 'final' (Metro-Roland, 2009). The sign itself, following Peirce's logic, can be broken down into three further categories: icon, index and symbol. A postcard or photograph of Uluru serves as an example of an icon because it resembles Uluru in sufficiently transparent ways (see Figure 2.2).

The same photograph of Uluru could also be regarded as a symbol however, because it is a place that is today regularly recalled as being the 'red heart' of Australia: it quite literally stands in for and symbolizes the spiritual heart of the country, but there are no connections between Uluru itself and 'the heart', other than shared cultural knowledge. In other words, to understand that symbolism requires the interpretant to have a degree of previous knowledge and experience of Uluru and its role within the national imagery of Australia (after Pennington & Thomsen, 2010). The same photograph is also indexical, to follow through with Peirce's logic, in that the photograph offers only a trace of the 'real' (Sturken & Cartwright, 2009).

Figure 2.2 Uluru (*Source:* Emma Waterton)

Dean MacCannell's work, *The Tourist* (1976; see also 1989), serves as an excellent and enduring example of a structuralist-inspired (particularly Peircean) exploration of the way tourists, as semioticians, understand and move through touristic spaces, which he sees as comprised of sight, marker and tourist. Reflecting back on Peirce's definition introduced earlier, which began with the suggestion that a sign is '...something which stands to somebody for something in some respect or capacity', we can see MacCannell's proposition working where 'something' becomes the marker, which represents 'something' (the sight) to somebody (the tourist) (van den Abbeele, 1980). Of particular interest here is MacCannell's typology of markers, which include signposts, interpretive panels and site guides/maps, all of which are *on*site, as well as postcards, familiarity, personal narratives, brochures and advertisement, all of which are found *off*site. These markers, MacCannell argues, often *make* the sights/sites in questions, and are used by visitors to legitimize, or not, those aspects of the site encountered in reality. How often, for example, have we heard our friends or family comment, upon their return, that Stonehenge, Mount Rushmore or the Colosseum, for example, 'was not as big as I was led to believe'. Indeed, MacCannell's assessment of touristic markers is more sophisticated still, incorporating five types or stages: naming, framing and elevating, enshrinement, mechanical reproduction and social reproduction (see van den Abbeele, 1980: 4). Of course, MacCannell's semiotic analysis does not occur only at the level of tourism sites and their communicative meaning to tourists. Rather, as MacCannell, himself, remarks:

> The more I examined my data, the more inescapable became my conclusion that tourist attractions are an unplanned typology of structures that provides direct access to the modern consciousness or 'world view'... (MacCannell, 1976: 2)

In this, a particular mode of communication allows MacCannell to make commentary upon broader structural relationships observable between the practices of tourism and modern society more generally. In other words, socio-cultural structures are here reflected in tourism (after Aitchison, 2000). At the same time that Saussurian-thinking was influencing the work of MacCannell, it was similarly migrating beyond the fields of linguistics and into cultural studies, marketing, sociology, anthropology and so forth, where it has become attached to a number of critical thinkers, including Roland Barthes and Claude Lévi-Strauss. Critically, this movement precipitated – or was precipitated by – a move away from assumptions that semiosis was the product of a static system, to that which saw it as unfolding in time; thinking which was key to the emergence of post-structuralist semiotic agendas.

Signs of the times: The post-structural 'crisis'

Whereas the structuralist approach emerged from concerns with *how* meaning is produced, post-structuralist-informed semiotic theories can be understood as agitating for the recognition and exploration of the effects and consequences of representations and their meanings. But, more than that, they also agitate for more nuanced understandings of *who* has the power to speak, and about what, thus drawing upon questions of power, politics, privilege and control. These, importantly, are relational questions, in that the power of some is held up against the loss of power or powerlessness of others, with semiotic analyses used to focus upon the techniques or modes of power that foster such an imbalance. In this, post-structuralist theories have had, and continue to have, profound effects on the way semiotic analyses are deployed, both within the field of heritage tourism and the social sciences and humanities more generally. These approaches, emerging in the 1980s and foregrounding the role of ideology, took serious issue with the *representation–reality* dualism so often invoked in structuralist renderings, particularly the assumption that '... naturally given and enduring meanings' were available, out there, and simply awaited their unlocking (Castree & MacMillan, 2004: 471; Scott, 2009: 351). Indeed, this reference to truth claims is one that post-structuralists, as a rule, simply have no interest in perpetuating. Instead, post-structuralist theorists see representations as developing within particular cultural systems, replete with power imbalances and representational dynamics that can, and do, affect the meanings that hold sway in those contexts. 'No signifier', as Dixon and Jones (2004: 88) point out, 'can be presumed to stand in a one-to-one relationship with a real-world referent'. Thus, if there is any binary opposition at play for this line of thinking, it is that which revolves around the logic between 'real' and 'represented', but only in so far as it is a binary that requires total deconstruction. As Scott goes on to argue:

> ... representations are never mirror-images of reality, but instead are always the product of diverse and ever-shifting contexts, and hence are never innocent, unbiased, or divorced from the realm of power and politics. (Scott, 2009: 351)

More often than not, those contexts that hold power are associated with the white, masculine and western gaze. Thus, while key proponents of post-structuralist thinking certainly include the likes of Michel Foucault and Jacques Derrida, it is also a style of deconstructionist thinking that has been strongly augmented by contributions from feminist and post-colonial approaches (see Butler, 1990; Said, 1978 as examples). But while scholars situated within both fields were quick to see the relevance of semiotic perspectives, they did so only with the assurances of key critical propositions. Central here was the rejection of binary oppositions and dualisms such as self/other, male/female, sex/gender, public/private and so forth, which are themselves underscored by notions of who ought to be considered 'centre', 'powerful', 'core', as opposed to 'marginalized', 'powerless' and 'peripheral' (Aitchison, 2000). Various explorations of postcards and travel brochures have unfolded along these lines, especially those examining constructions of 'the Other' as exotic, foreign, distant (see Albers & James, 1988; Enloe, 1989).

Another key element of this style of thinking has been the idea of discourse, a term that ranges in use from references to the organization of sentences in a linguistic sense, to that of discourse as a regulating body that forms consciousness. Post-structuralist accounts of discourse, particularly those underpinned by the work of Foucault (1970, 1977, 1984, 2003), are grounded in social and cultural contexts, and extend beyond conceptualizations of 'language-in-use'. Rather than take discourse as a straightforward vehicle of meaning, which is reflective and neutral, such accounts understand it to be more powerful and situated (Blommaert, 2005: 2; Taylor, 2001: 6–7). This understanding looks beyond structuralist theories of semiotics to focus on the potency of discourse. Importantly, this grounds discourse within societal processes, as well as revealing the recursive relationships discourses share with ideology and knowledge. As Lazar (2000: 376) points out, a useful way of conceptualizing this understanding of discourse is to think of it as a '"meaning potential" ... that enables and constrains possible ways of knowing about the world, a sense of who we may (and may not be) within that world order, and how we may (or may not) relate to one another'.

In many ways, the turn to discourse in the 1980s was symptomatic of the times, as language and representations, on the back of dissatisfaction with structuralist approaches, had become politicized and critical issues in contemporary society. This was fuelled primarily by a cynicism and distrust of the ways in which language and representations had been regulated and ritualized, not only in policy but in practice too, where it was seen as a tool used to propagate exclusion and marginalization, excisions, cuts and absences. The prevalence and growing visibility of the media played a crucial role in this, particularly in terms of its calculated manipulation by a range of political parties. This is as true of the heritage and tourism sectors as it is of any other area of social life, where talk no longer circulates around whether there *are* problems surrounding heritage tourism and what they may be, but how those problems may best be interpreted and tackled (Hajer, 1995: 14). New Labour's attempts to tackle issues of social exclusion in the United

Kingdom during the last decade are a useful case in point, playing out in the heritage sector precisely in ways that failed to problematize the *idea* of heritage and instead set about increasing visitor numbers to those sites understood as heritage within dominant articulations by way of solution (see Waterton, 2010b for a fuller exploration). Perhaps the biggest concession in this regard was the move to subtly change the language we use to talk about the past, which moved from 'heritage' to the 'historic environment', in an endeavour seeking to remove any negative connotations from the field of management. It was a sleight-of-hand, and in this context both the 'problem' and its solutions became discursive.

All this is based on the assumption that discourse *constitutes* certain knowledge, values, identities, consciousnesses and relationships, and is *constitutive* in the sense of not only sustaining and legitimizing the status quo, but in transforming it too. As such, at the heart of post-structuralist accounts of semiotics lies the impression that representations move beyond the provision of description and are instead envisaged as interpretations, educators and constructors of meaning. Taking up a definition such as this makes clear that the way we 'talk about', or represent, things unfolds in three clear ways: it defines the identities and subject positions from which we make our 'talk'; it constructs and mediates the ways we act and organize; and it produces and maintains the knowledge and beliefs that in turn work to sustain and legitimize that way of 'talking' (Fairclough *et al.*, 2004: 2; Marston, 2004: 36). Post-structuralist approaches to semiotic theory are thus critical in the sense that they test the opacity between the 'real' and the 'perceived' in an attempt to explore the promotion of ideology and the consolidation of hegemony. Following this logic through, representations became indicative of particular storylines or discourses, and are used to represent and understand the world in certain ways. This sort of semiotic analysis would tend towards a vigorous assessment of how language practically figures in constructions and understandings of the world that surrounds us, with the explicit aim of elucidating a sense of not only how a discourse is being used but *why*.

An important consequence of the post-structuralist imagining is that the plethora of resultant discourse ensures that forms are always competing against one another for dominance, power and control (after Foucault, 1980: 35). In short, within society certain discourses are more powerful than others. This is not to deny the power of agency in terms of the reception of discourse; rather, the point here is that there is a need to unpack the subtle means by which agents *make* themselves into subjects through discursive features. An obvious example would be the legal codes that prescribe the boundaries of operation in everyday life. There are, however, far subtler discourses that function to maintain perceptions and attitudes. Waterton (2009,

2010b, 2013), for instance, has examined the exclusionary discourses operating within the British heritage tourism industry. By practising certain modes of exclusionary discourse, which often revolve around the use of pronouns 'we', 'us' and 'them', heritage organizations in Britain can be shown to participate and propagate in a discourse of a dominating, white and overwhelmingly middle-class heritage, which is peddled to a range of social groups gripped by the realities of exclusion. In more overly tourism terms, Carla Almeida Santos sums-up this post-structuralist agenda as:

> Media-created narratives are highly selective, highlighting the beautiful and exotic, and often grounded in a structure of opposites such as ancient versus modern, and corrupted versus unadulterated. Viewed this way, coverage of destinations and hosts promotes misrepresentation – a world of the Other as the writer wants it to be and the travel editor believes it should be. (Almeida Santos, 2004: 126)

Dann (1986), Feighery (2009), Metusela and Waitt (2012), Morgan and Pritchard (1998), Urry (1990, 2002) and Waterton (2009, 2013) have all undertaken studies that would comfortably fall within this sort of semiotic analysis, principally because of the attention they place upon issues of dominance and persuasion. What distinguishes these approaches from structuralist readings of representation defined by de Saussure, is that movement from a purer form of linguistics to a broader exploration of power, context and history (Hall, 1997). John Urry's work in *The Tourist Gaze* is perhaps most emblematic of this style of analysis, especially given his considered attention to Foucault's panopticism and notions of 'the gaze' as key formations in relations of power within the tourism sector. Of course, given his overall choice of terminology Urry's adherence to Foucauldian thinking is unsurprising, and springs from an account of knowledge that is both socially constructed and constructing (Aitchison, 1999). Though Urry maintains MacCannell's structural ontology, which accounts for a theorization of tourism built around familiar binaries, he is in many other ways offering readers a rejection of structuralist approaches to the visual, in particular by seeking to mythicize notions of a 'pure and innocent eye' (Larsen & Urry, 2011: 1110). As part of this criticality, he presents a sharp analysis of specific tourism practices, which he uses to also shed light on Foucauldian relations of power. Here, Urry (1990) constructs his tourist 'gaze' as one that is organized by professionals and institutions – via different, dominant discourses – and simmers in touristic spaces, layering them with socially constructed messages and realizations.

What is problematic about this rendering for our own semiotic landscape, as pointed out by Haldrup and Larsen (2006), is that such a formulation of the gaze never takes into account the ways in which the practices of tourism 'touch' and 'interact' with the body. As Haldrup and Larsen go on to argue:

> Natural surroundings and objects are seen as signifying social constructs that can be unveiled through authoritative semiotic readings rather than in terms of how they are used and lived within practice ... This partly reflects the fact that in the social sciences culture is conventionally treated as something mental and human, a 'way of life' without thingness, occupying the minds of people and their social representations. (Haldrup & Larsen, 2006: 277)

Like Urry, Morgan and Pritchard (1998: 146) similarly draw attention to the less-than-innocent role played by representations, arguing that any visual expression of tourism is inevitably already enmeshed with wider historical, cultural, social, economic and political processes. And these processes *always*, inevitably, intervene in representations (Castree & MacMillan, 2004). In postcolonial contexts, destination images play a particularly powerful role, acting as cues that signify an authorized process of self/othering, for example, making claims about such places as if they have captured their essence (after Castree & MacMillan, 2004; see Amoamo & Thompson, 2010). As Lane and Waitt (2001) have suggested, tourism can therefore be imagined as an influential, formative process through which particular narratives about a nation's past become *known* and *familiar* to its subjects. Following from this, a critical seam of research has developed that questions the tendency within many contexts to produce and package essentialized and disempowering images of the marginalized, the local, the Indigenous, the subjugated, the less powerful and so forth. In the Australian context, for example, work by Chris Healy (2008), Rebecca Lawrence and Chris Gibson (2007), Mary O'Dowd (2009), Libby Porter (2010) and Peter Read (2000) among others, has demonstrated the degree to which a particular rendering of Aboriginality and culture have come to permeate all aspects of social life with deeply entrenched cultural inconsistencies and insecurities that recursively plague Australia's self-image. This is an example of what Castree and MacMillan (2004: 475) label the silent, certain violence of representation, predicated 'by arresting the relational flux of the world'. What these sorts of analyses have been crucial for pointing out is that heritage tourism sites, and tourism sites more generally, while polysemic, are appropriated, used and produced in the name of any number of ideological exercises. What is important about this assessment is that it opens up the way for us to consider how visitors, too, bring with them their own sets of discourses, those which are also brought to bear upon the heritage sites in question.

Signs of the times: A 'more-than' semiotics

While the previous two sections examined the 'how' and 'why' of meaning-making, we want to add to this an exploration of the 'doing', which necessarily entails concerning ourselves with an 'affective' approach. Yet 'affect', like many words circulating academia, carries multiple meanings and connotations. As is the case with terms such as 'identity', 'community', 'culture' and 'discourse', it conjures up a range of meanings and potentialities, and thus warrants something by way of definition. For this we borrow from the work of Ben Anderson (2006: 735), who explains that affect is '... a transpersonal capacity which a body has to be affected (through an affection) and to affect (as the result of modifications)'. This understanding is very much invested with the earlier work of Deleuze, Guattari, Spinoza and Massumi, which, as Anderson goes on to argue, emerges from:

> ... a processual logic of transitions that take place during spatially and temporally distributed encounters in which 'each transition is accompanied by a variation in capacity: a change in which powers to affect and be affected are addressable by a next event and how readily addressable they are'. (Massumi, 2002a: 15; cited in Anderson, 2006: 735)

What this allows in the context of this volume is the development of the argument that semiotic analyses can, and should, be applied to 'other-than' representational contexts, such as performances, the non-verbal, the multisensory, ritual, gestures, movements and emergent experiences. The third element of our semiotic landscape, which adds to our structural and discursive accounts, is a post-structuralist rendering that stresses corporeal engagements and proximities. But how does this flow from the previous two sections? Perhaps the most cited illustrative example of structuralist thinking, which comes in the form of 'the traffic light as sign-system', goes some way towards answering this. Most of us, for example, are able to recognize the meaning signalled by the colour 'red', which conveys to us the need to stop. This is a neat example of structuralist thinking. From there, we might begin to wonder *who* determined the correlation of meanings between the colours 'red', 'amber' and 'green' and the attributed meanings of 'stop', 'caution' and 'go', as the relationships between them are, of course, entirely arbitrary. Who, then, determined what those colours would signify, and on what authority, are questions someone with a post-structuralist agenda might consider. Our turn to 'affect' emerges from reflections upon our own reactions to that sign-system in our everyday lives: remember, for example, the intensity of bodily feelings that are engendered if you have ever run a red light *by accident*. Anxiety levels spike immediately, and we are flooded, quite literally, with feelings of horror and disbelief, often before our conscious-self has properly begun to articulate the issue. We digest it all *already in concert* with an awareness of our bodily responses – the quickened heart, the intake of breath, the widening eyes, the tension. How to capture this fuller complexity of a sign-system, complete with reflections upon its affects and consequences?

Our foray into this sort of examination is linked with a general dissatisfaction with the privileging of the visual in semiotic analyses. Although our position can easily be linked with a form of social constructivism, our suggestion is that we need to think about processes of signification and meaning-making as occurring within action and interactions – with other people and the world around us, rather than solely within the representational dimensions of discourse and structures of symbolic orders (after Anderson & Harrison, 2010: 2). In this, we slide into a way of thinking, or perhaps a way of thought or *thinking* about thinking, that brings together cognition with impulse, intuition and habit, with no easy way of cleaving them apart. This is a way of thinking most often characterized as non-or more-than-representational (see Watson & Waterton, 2013, for a fuller account).

'*Non*-representational' thinking is often linked with human geographer Nigel Thrift, perhaps its most cited proponent, who has characterized the approach as a response to the deadening of geographical thinking or, as John Wylie (2007: 163) puts it, the draining 'of life out of things', triggered by too avid a focus on representations. For Thrift, there are three principal problems with dominant representational approaches: the implication of distance, a desire for codification and the prioritization of speech, cognition and vision (see Castree & MacMillan, 2004). As Wolff (2012: 10) goes on to argue, collectively these have rendered invisible all manner of things that are central, important, to human life, such as experience, emotion, affect. Indeed, as Tim Ingold (1995: 58) so eloquently puts it:

> '[s]omething [...] must be wrong somewhere, if the only way to understand our own creative involvement in the world is by taking ourselves out of it'. (Ingold, 1995: 58)

The lines of inquiry carved out in this section thus dovetail with critiques of the broader social sciences' and humanities' focus on 'representation', which have gained considerable strength over the last decade, so much so that, as Christopher Prendergast (2000: ix) has colourfully pointed out, it is now 'a concept in ruins, carpet bombed by the formidable arsenals of contemporary critical theory'. To remedy this, Prendergast suggests we are in need of a:

> ... renewal of a different, and more judicious, kind of reflexive turning back on the concept, something more sensitive to complexity and ambiguity than the catchphrases ('against' representation or, in even more naive register, 'beyond' representation) that, like so many camp followers, have pitched camp in the debris left by the scorched-earth policy. (Prendergast, 2000: ix)

His is a call to finesse rather than deconstruct; augment, rather than supersede. The net result, as Whatmore (1999: 29) pointed out some time ago, should be the extension of post-structuralist concerns so as to encompass '... all kinds of unspeakable "message bearers" and material processes, such as technical devices, instruments and graphics, and bodily capacities, habits and skills'. The impulse behind these attempts to revitalize representational analysis thus lies in the belief that there are meanings and affects tangled up with them that both precede and exceed 'the signifying regime of ideological systems' (Spinks, 2001: 23; cited in Wolff, 2012: 10). Viewed specifically in terms of our own project, the turn to more-than- or other-than-representation becomes an attempt to fill a gap in the literature, a gap that has heretofore been constrained by a propensity towards working up classifications and typologies of heritage 'attractions' and 'tourists' without making any real attempts to understand what actually happens in moments of encounter. It is thus an approach that sits in contradistinction to the well-explored world of the tourism marketer as purveyor of meaning (see Chapter 4), and revolves around the emergence of an interest in the politics of affect. Affect, as a theoretical concept, is one that is transpersonal and mobile, always in flow from one body to another in response to atmosphere, mood and so forth (Pile, 2010). Perhaps Teresa Brennan (2004: 1) sums this up best when she asks if there is anyone '... who has not, at least once, walked into a room and "felt the atmosphere"'? Her point is that affect is communicable, at times spreading like wildfire; but it is not necessarily 'speakable'. Rather, it moves around – from body, to object, to place, to body – as a form of contagion, and circulates, but often in ways that are ineffable.

That said, it is a concept that is charged with taking both the social and biology seriously and simultaneously, and does so via specific conceptualizations of the body. This is a 'body', however, that is not confined to social constructions only but is driven, too, by biological impulses that are pre- and non-cognitive (Pile, 2010: 8). In fact, it is a concept that is doubly located, as Clive Barnett (2008: 188) points out: first, it hints at the relational interactions *between* bodies and places; and second, it talks also of those impulses and nerve-firings that sit *within* bodies, just below mindful consciousness. The first is inflected with notions of external circulation, whereas the latter is concerned with what actually happens, biologically, within the body. Thus while social in origin, affect is also *bodily felt*, as Brennan (2004: 1) argues, and 'literally gets into the individual'. It will not, of course, climb into each 'body' in quite the same way. Thus, while different heritage tourism sites will attempt to construct distinct touristic messages, visitors will not necessarily be affected by them similarly – some will reflect, some will reject, others still will feel bored or simply disengaged, and some will ignore the touristic messages entirely and simply respond to the object itself or to the other people who are there, their friends, their partners, their children or the presence of strangers in a crowd.

Thinking back to the example of Uluru, one might start to wonder how our proximity to different narratives plays out, not only in terms of affect, but in terms of power and politics too. Here, analyses of what people *do* when they are trying to make sense of their reactions to the narratives on display tell us something about affect. This is because, as Gorton (2007: 342, original emphasis) points out, 'the body both participates in and acts out emotion. Our feelings are not just registered in our conscious awareness but are *felt* and enacted by our bodies'. The geometries of power brought to bear by post-structuralist thinking does not disappear in this participation. Rather, those bodies move and interact in all their gendered, racialized, aged and classed ways. Uluru, like all other sites of heritage tourism, is laced with complex relations of power, not all of which are uniformly distributed. We visit such sites with the same bodies with which we move through life: if we are already resisting marginalization, we do so still as a visitor, as a tourist. Each site is distinctive and will thus have its own distinctive interpretation. And within those interpretations are implicit affective affordances that speak more directly to some visitors than others. At Uluru, only particular grammars of the body are recognized, such that if an Australian 'settler' narrative is pulled into view and remembered, other, Indigenous, alternatives slip away and are forgotten. What we are interested in here are the tools that heritage tourism sites afford some visitors – that confidence or a feeling of having the *right* to fill its spaces – and not others. Do some visitors pull back in defence or shame while others performatively engage that history with pride? Are they viscerally aware of their proximity or distance? How are people quite literally *positioned* in these dynamics, and how are these positions felt and configured as a consequence of the affect that is afforded and available in that space?

Based on this theorizing, it should become clear that developing a non- or more-than-representational semiotic theory for heritage tourism warrants the adoption of an approach that concerns itself with 'doing', 'performing', 'framing', 'producing' and 'acting', emphasizing the '... flow of practice in everyday life as embodied, as caught up with and committed to the creation of affect, as contextual, and as *technologised* through language and objects...' (Thrift & Dewsbury, 2000: 415, original emphasis). Although a steady stream of work on affect continues to emerge from cultural studies, human geographers and feminist theorists (Gorton, 2007; Gregg & Seigworth, 2010; Pile, 2010; Thien, 2005; Thrift, 2004), it remains one that has had little impact on the field of heritage tourism (with the exception of Crouch, 2000, 2010a; Crouch et al., 2001; Girman, 2012; Knudsen & Waade, 2010; Lane & Waitt, 2001; Little, 2010; Obrador Pons, 2003; Paschen, 2010). The volume of work produced by David Crouch, and more recently Kenneth Little (2010), stands out in contradistinction here, owing to Crouch's continuing theoretical push towards notions of encounter, and his merging of representations and lived heritage, which, he argues, '... are constituted in merging flows of living' (2010b: 18). Representations, in this theorizing, are embodied and lived:

> ... drawn into a felt 'doing' and knowledge-in-practice in what Shotter calls a contingent process of figuring out the world through intersubjective practices, practical knowledge, learnt, acquired and wrestled with, having the potential to reconfigure our sense of the world and how things are done and our position in relation to them ... (Crouch et al., 2001: 262).

Likewise, Little (2010), inspired by the work of Kathleen Stewart, traces practices of affirmative augmentation and affective encounter in moments of touristic engagement in Belize. While this is undoubtedly an emerging area of theoretical endeavour, there is as yet not a full complement of research in this area (but see recent publications such as Girman, 2012; Little, 2010; Waterton & Watson, 2013). Given that affect can be used to infer cultural and social expression, both of which are central to the heritage tourist's experience, this is something we hope to engender. The proposition underpinning this volume is that the boundaries of the photographic imagery, and performances of photography itself, offer a means by which to tackle affect within the field of heritage tourism, though other dimensions of experience would suffice also. This is because each photograph brings with it the photographing body, along with those bodies and any other non-human elements that may be *in* the photo, as well as those who will view its results (Robinson & Picard, 2009). What this means is taking the ubiquitous touristic practice of photography beyond notions of representation, which is done by considering their affective intensities and their ability, not only to signify but to be felt, bringing with it two interesting consequences (Larsen, 2005; Latham & McCormack, 2009: 253). The first of these is that photography should no longer be considered a straightforward representation of reality, instead becoming something implicit to the creation of new realities (Crang, 1997; Edensor, 2001; Larsen, 2005; Scarles, 2009). The second is that scholars now need to bring to the fore an understanding of tourists themselves, particularly in terms of their active, corporeal, expressive and engaged involvement in the creation and framing of images (Garrod, 2009; Larsen, 2005; Scarles, 2009) (see Figure 2.3).

Implicit within both of these propositions is the assumption that the power of the photograph lies with its ability to '...arrest time and make memories'; that is, the taking of a photograph provides, as Haldrup and Larsen (2003: 39; see also Hsiu-yen Yeh, 2009) go on to argue, embodied performances sustained within complex assemblages that articulate together a range of bodies, technologies, images, scripts and practices, all working to create 'desired future memory'. The meshing together of tourism, heritage and photography is of course nothing new, but here we intend to push the

Figure 2.3 The photographing body (*Source:* Emma Waterton)

latter beyond the representational modes most often afforded it. This is a central theme for the volume, and is one that will be unpacked in far greater detail in Chapters 5 and 6.

Conclusion

The journey from structuralism to the more-than-representational realm of everyday life very much encapsulates what we are trying to achieve in this book, and our own research in various parts of the world, both individually and as collaborators, has reflected its emergent concerns. Like everyone labelled with that rather unsatisfactory word 'tourist', we have variously responded to representations, been affected by our surroundings and been moved to feelings of wonder and amazement by the places we have visited. But these common responses have profoundly influenced our approach to this book. If semiotics is a way of understanding the construction of meaning, and if it is a good way of understanding meaning in heritage tourism, then maybe it has value beyond and as well as text and representation. How far can we then take it into the realm of experience and forms of engagement that employ every sense and make us react as bodies and with capacities for sentient expression, emotion and imagination? The act of photography brings bodies and objects together and the act of creating a photograph – a representation – is a culmination of that bodily encounter, a moment of positioning, balance and distancing, a moment where the body itself quite literally 'holds sway'. And yet in doing so, it expresses an emotional intensity that culminates in the photograph, an intensity that might only exist because of a pre-existing representational order. It is easy to see why the image in general, and the photograph in particular, exists at the centre of touristic semiosis, but its context has a much more expansive cartography than the one it represents in its rectangular frame, and that bigger picture – the semiotic landscape of heritage tourism – is the subject of this book.

3 Signing the Past

The previous chapter historicized the arrival of a semiotic mode of enquiry in relation to heritage tourism, exploring both representational (representations, constructs, products) and more-than-representational (affect and emotion) theories. This is because we seek to draw explanatory value from all of these perspectives in order to develop a new understanding of the semiotics of heritage tourism. Our purpose in this chapter is to narrow that focus and explore the symbolic meaning constructed around heritage itself, placing emphasis on how a consideration of symbolic meaning connects with deeper understandings of personal, local, regional and national pasts. Accordingly, the chapter takes as its focus the semiotic landscape that is constituted in, and by, heritage tourism attractions. Individually, these landscapes or 'imaginaria' contain the representations, responses and meanings that make heritage both understood and felt, and which establish the relationships between heritage objects and the people who encounter them. Our concept of semiotics in heritage thus encompasses not only its visual sign systems, but also its genealogies and ways of 'doing', feeling and experiencing. We are concerned, therefore, not only with representations, constructs and products, but also with all those subjective engagements – both cognitive and affective – that complete the experience.

In terms of argumentation, this chapter is based on the proposition that the semiotics of heritage can either diminish and restrict its meaning and significance to a limited rendering of the past, or provide a means for individual and subjective engagements that may well be unrelated to, or even stand in opposition with, the attenuated semiosis associated with official, authorized or commodified discourses. Illuminating the tensions between these positions, along with the cultural symbols that might support or thwart them, is our intention from this point forwards. By the close of this chapter, we hope to have laid the groundwork for this process, but to do that we need to present our understanding of heritage as a social imaginary of the past and a semiotic landscape replete with cultural meaning.

Cultural Context and Cultural Process

Several years ago now, Dean MacCannell (1976: 43–44; see also Haldrup & Bærenholdt, in press) famously stated that there were few sights in modernity that carried the self-proclaiming powers of the seven wonders of the ancient world; little that were so spectacular in themselves that they did not require institutional support to mark them off as attractions. Most attractions, to follow MacCannell's line of thought, are therefore social constructions that require the distinguishing adjective 'extraordinary' as defined by culturally determined and conventional representational codes (Rojek, 1997: 70). The process by which this institutional support develops around an object creates the first basis of what we refer to as a 'semiotic landscape'. In this process, heritage converges with place, and in that convergence discourses about the past emerge with representations that have semiotic qualities. However, in developing this theme, we will argue that semiotic landscapes also provide contexts for more- and other-than-representational moments, in addition to their representational codifications. Indeed, such landscapes are effectively created in moments by people and objects *doing* things – before, during and after their visit – as well as the representations that construct *a priori* meanings in, and about, those places. This landscape may be discernible only at a micro-level, containing only a person and an object. Alternatively, it may have some broader resonance, such as a system of representation that may impinge on it. Finally, the landscape may be noticeable through the 'discourses in place', as Scollon and Scollon (2003) describe the socio-historically formed discursive formations that mediate such engagements. An example of such a discursive formation is Laurajane Smith's (2006) 'Authorized Heritage Discourse', to which we referred earlier as a systematic representation of socio-cultural significances that uses heritage to attach meaning to national identity and other socio-cultural phenomena. Though Smith is referring only to a particular way of seeing, experiencing and understanding heritage, her point is that this has become so powerful, so pervasive, that it is accepted as common sense by the population in general. Mitch Rose (2002) has made similar observations about the Giza pyramids in Egypt, which he regards as a hegemonic and referential touchstone. Such was the degree of the symbolic import connected to the term 'heritage', in that context, that it came to '... set the terms of debate .... It was a word whose definition never needed explaining and was never questioned' (Rose, 2002: 464). Though writing much earlier, Culler alludes to a similar discursive context in emphasizing the semiotic connections between individual sights and the production of knowledge:

The production of touristic sights relies on semiotic mechanisms whose operation may seem quite local and contingent, but the general framework and product of these signifying mechanisms, the touristic code, is a modern consensus of vast scope, a systematized, value-laden knowledge of the world. (Culler, 1990: 10)

There are linearities in these descriptions of semiotic practice that become strained however, when we consider them in light of new and emerging theory. It could be argued, for example, that a semiotic landscape need not be linked exclusively to authorized or systematized values attached to particular physical places at all, or, if it is, it may be formed there contingently from the evanescent mobilities of its actors (Bærenholdt et al., 2004). Fleeting semiotic landscapes are constituted, for example, in a temporary exhibition in a museum or gallery, a musical performance, a conversation that evokes memories or the pasts of others, cartographies of meaning carried along in streams of knowledge and experience, on beaches, among ruins or on the streets. Imaginaria that are not physically emplaced might include engagements with media, such as books, magazines or their digital e-counterparts, websites and broadcast media, or they may simply be the evocations carried bodily, of memory, dislocated thoughts or emotional attachments, promptings and rememberings. More than this, semiotic landscapes may collide and interact, or they may be the result of such collisions, interactions and coincidences. A flood of memories may be released in a moment of engagement with a place or an object, a photograph found while looking for something else, or a long forgotten scent carried on the potted air of a train carriage.

On the other hand, more stable situations do clearly occur where, with repetition and regularity, patterns of response form or crystallize into a representational system or the site of engagement, to which Scollon and Scollon (2003) refer as a 'nexus' and which in its systemic manifestations is susceptible to semiotic analysis. For example, Washington Irving's (1832) account of his 'discovery' of the Alhambra is replete with romantic affect, yet before the end of the century it was a national monument and firmly part of the tourist trail. Likewise, MacCannell's (1976: 43–48) concept of *sight sacralization* and the search for fugitive authenticities reflects similar processes. For us, however, semiotic landscapes also have an elusive and imaginary quality reflective of Crouch's (2010b) notion of a sensing of heritage that is situational and emergent, and referring to senses including, but also going well beyond, the visual, which may evoke affective as well as represented feeling or expressed emotion on the part of the subject.

In the end, we are interested in the effects of all of these things, both on the individual and on the individual's encounters with others, in the semiotic landscape of heritage tourist attractions. And while we are not necessarily looking for *systematic* meaning formation in the context of heritage tourism, we are interested in the effects of that context, which may be meaningful in a sustained way, or in the moment, or not meaningful at all because they are not sensed as such. In this we pay due respect to the theoretical formulations described in later chapters, including mobilities theory, actor network theory, non-representational theory and Fairclough's notion of 'semiotic modalities' (2008: 163), and yet we are keen to retain a more open approach, a semiotic *landscape* in which we seek a variety of effects, engagements and relationalities. In essence, our interest in critical heritage studies moves us to some key focal points that have always been a part of discourse analysis, such as the relationship between text and context and, more particularly for us, engaging with the exposure, role and position of power and national identity in the semiotic landscape of heritage tourism. This *critical* imagination sustains our interest in the deconstructive potentialities of text and visual culture (Waterton & Watson, 2010; see also Crouch & Lübbren, 2003; Schirato & Webb, 2004).

A further basis for the semiotic landscape in heritage tourism is a corresponding interest in what Kirshenblatt-Gimblett (1998: 17–79) refers to as *agencies of display*, which in a kind of subtle reciprocity both respond to and sustain the scopic regimes that are often characteristic of a semiotic landscape (Jay, 1988, 1996; Metz, 1977; Watson & Waterton, 2010a). This agency may be found in practice in the activities of heritage tourism operators, marketing communications and the design of sites, all of which can be understood representationally and visually and, as a result, can be critically deconstructed to reveal aspects of their performativity and practice, including certain cultural concerns, anxieties, identities, ideologies and concomitant power relations. There is nothing new about this; it is a basic application of Western Marxist structural analysis and typically reveals social and cultural phenomena in hegemonic formations.

In tourism studies, the visual semiotic landscape is actively sought and well documented in the images and texts that are generated by operators and destination managers, and many of these productions represent official heritage values of one sort or another (Waterton 2009, 2010a). Thus, brochures, guidebooks, postcards and other media provide rich pickings for the tourism semiotician and have done so for some time (see Hughes, 1998; Marwick, 2001; Morgan & Pritchard, 1998). The heritage sector has attracted particular attention for its dependence on visual display and its use of such display in the discursive contexts of heritage as a cultural process rather than merely a collection of objects (Smith, 2006; Waterton, 2013; Waterton & Watson, 2010). The emphasis on the visual in such semiotic encounters and academic analyses reveals some interesting perspectives on the 'secret work' of heritage objects (Watson & Waterton, 2010a) in giving substance to what they signify and making visible and tangible the narratives they support. This in turn substantiates meaning in their context (see Haldrup & Bærenholdt, in press). So, in effectively aestheticizing cultural products, their tangibility masks an active ideological role, creating experts, connoisseurs and professionals who make this special knowledge their own and exchange it in commodifications of various kinds. We have to be experts before we can talk authoritatively about English country houses and their contents, for example, or of the ubiquitous medieval church and castle, the paintings of Velasquez or antique mirrors; and if we do talk authoritatively about these objects then we must have become an expert, if only an amateur one – or so the assumption goes. In other words, professional experts have come to *own*, in a sense, the objects of the past *through* their tangibility and visuality. This in turn excites the attention of the non-expert majority, validates expert knowledge and substantiates the exclusive and univocal discourses of heritage that underpin class-based interests and power relations (Waterton, 2009: 37; see Waterton, 2010b for further discussion).

In tandem with the critique levelled at 'official' and 'authorized' representations of heritage tourism sites and their narratives, scholars have also started to explore the concomitant spaces opened up by an interest in their audiences. While once it was assumed that such visitors played a silent, passive role, few scholars today would accept such a proposition. Perhaps this is the case more than ever, given that we operate in a media-saturated, individual-orientated culture. That said, there clearly remains, at the core of all this practice, a dominant, hegemonic expression of heritage, it is just that we need to think through how it works, not just what it is. Something must be sustaining hegemonic discourses – somewhere, somehow – because they are clearly effective and acted upon, shaping practice and conduct in semiotic landscapes and beyond. There can be little doubt that visual display and the intense materiality that supports it is, in itself, sustaining, in that it provides empirical and experiential evidence of, and for, the discourse with which it is functionally and reciprocally enmeshed:

> Our connections with the past are largely tangible, or have a materiality upon which they depend that makes them objects of heritage, and it is visual culture that lends these objects the means of representation and achievement of meaning. (Watson & Waterton, 2010b: 2)

Nevertheless, while the visual appears to predominate in representations, we have to consider other forms of practice and experience, and we must consider these both within, and as part of, the contexts of meaning, the semiotic landscapes of heritage tourism. As we have suggested, enough has been written and is emergent in the fields from which heritage studies sources its theory to suggest there is more at play here than the visual and the representational, however important these are. In order to do justice, therefore, to the semiotic landscapes of heritage tourism, we will look at them as complex imaginaria, the loci of emergent meanings concerning the past and the relationalities of people, places and heritage objects. More will come of this in later chapters. Before that, however, we need to consider the temporalities of heritage, its historical construction and its development in relation to specific places, attractions or categories of heritage attraction. We refer to these temporalities as the *genealogies of heritage*, and by this we mean the historical contexts and processes that have prepared and conditioned certain objects and places as heritage and therefore as objects of heritage tourism.

The Genealogies of Heritage Tourism

As Coleman and Crang have suggested:

> ... [t]here is nothing natural about a tourist attraction. Very often the toured are marked out as possessing a culture defined as an organic totality, fixed in a place. The local culture is seen as evolving through collective activity, production and reproduction. Local tradition is disrupted by outside forces. Indigenous culture, and especially folk culture, is thus framed a non-modern activity. (Coleman & Crang, 2002: 6)

Nowhere, we argue, is this more pronounced than in that category of tourism known as heritage tourism. Here, like other tourist attractions, heritage tourism sites, places and landscapes depend on some well-established and quite specific semiotic processes, processes that are linked not only to practices of visual representations more generally, but the visualities of *heritage* too. We have already referred to Dean MacCannell's concept of *sight sacralization*, by which 'sites' become 'sights' in a process that is comprised of four core components: the attraction, the tourist, the sight itself and a marker (a sign or system of signs) that indicates the touristic significance of the sight in its cultural context. David Harvey (2001) has placed this in an historical context that is more sharply focused on heritage by observing that every society has a relationship with its past, expressed in the meaning and nature of its uses in the present. With this in mind, Harvey charts the long-term trajectory of heritage as a set of relationships between pasts and presents, concluding that in avoiding the 'presentness' of much heritage thinking, a more rounded analysis of its embedded and contingent nature could be derived and applied to understandings of its role in the production of identity, power and authority. As well as providing a cogent analysis of the temporal depth of heritage as a set of relationships and processes, Harvey also provides us with an opportunity to consider specific genealogies of heritage that have, over time, accreted around certain places, objects and, indeed, ideas. He goes on to argue that these are not necessarily the product of late 20th century, post-industrial cultural shifts; rather, there is a longer antecedence. The important point for us, however, is that there is a temporal context for heritage or, to put it another way, a *history of heritage*, to borrow from Harvey, that provides a range of genealogies and the substance and momentum of heritage practices, including the formation of attraction value and tourism.

In this way, the genealogies of heritage tourism contribute to the semiotic landscape of heritage objects and are formative in creating touristic interest in them. It can be said that the historic and socio-cultural forces that have shaped practice in and around a heritage tourist attraction, condition in a performative way what is expected from, and experienced at, a heritage site. The signifiers that owe something to that genealogy may be sought in both the representational and more-than-representational aspects of a site, and what is thus known and felt about it. Our interest here, representation, is concerned with the visual, and thus includes a variety of texts, narratives and media. Along similar lines, Bell and Lyall (2002: 24) have drawn attention to the way that artistic representations of particular vistas have, since the 19th century, worked their way into the status of icons of cultural identity that are then captured in postcards and commercial travel brochures. Feeling in this context relates to both emotion – as something that is expressed within the self and to others – and to affect, which, though felt, is not consciously expressable without entering the realms of the representational, as discussed in the previous chapter.

Some examples may serve here to demonstrate both the temporal depth of heritage signification, as suggested by Harvey (2001), and the contemporary nature of heritage as a process. Reflections on the United Kingdom serve our point well, as there one of the official agencies of heritage itself, English Heritage, is the clear result of a particular view of what constitutes heritage and how it should be represented (Waterton, 2010b). The particular genealogy of heritage in that context is thrown into sharp relief by its singular inability to address political agendas based around notions of inclusivity that are, in reality, attempts to assimilate cultural diversity around an existing authorized heritage discourse. This discourse is itself, in the United Kingdom at least, another formation of the history of its heritage. Heritage – as it is understood, represented and consumed there – is the result of several centuries of attention and defining activity, and it is difficult to understand these processes without some recognition of their antecedents, as Harvey (2001: 321) has pointed out in discussing the pre-modern contexts of heritage.

Our reflections thus begin with early antiquarians, such as Leland in the 16th century (Chandler, 1993), Camden and Aubrey in the 17th and Stukeley in the 18th, all of whom did much to frame and elevate the constituent materiality of heritage – its monumentality – and link it to an emerging concept of 'the nation'. Camden's Britannia, first published (in Latin) in 1588, was printed in English well into the 18th century, such was its authority (Schnapp, 1996: 140). It is interesting, in relation to the nation-forming uses of heritage, that Camden was reluctant to ascribe very much of what he saw to the prehistoric period and sought, rather, to find the antecedents of Britannia in its more culturally appealing Roman remains. In this context, heritage was used to link an emerging but uncertain sense of national identity with the power of Rome, made tangible in its archaeology (or any archaeology), which was entirely apposite to the emergence of a new empire that would seek to overshadow its predecessor in terms of culture, governance and global ambition (Clark, 1965: 28).

It was not until William Stukeley's travels in the following century, however, that many prehistoric and Roman monuments were comprehensively listed and classified. His interest in prehistoric monuments, such as Stonehenge and Avebury, was stoked by a growing obsession with matters druidical as an essentially British heritage that was, to his mind, related (rather conveniently) to early Christianity (Piggott, 1989: 143–146). Here is early evidence of the tangibility of the past in the form of monuments and earthworks visible in the landscape, providing substance for a particular heritage discourse that had a clear historical and political purpose. In this sense, Stukeley was engaged in the construction of a national heritage that supported both a distinct British identity and an avowedly anti-Catholic religious position (Harvey, 2001: 334).

The 18th century also provided a prefiguration of the cultural elevation of the medieval in the aesthetics of the picturesque. This concept of a landscape with buildings was celebrated particularly in the work of William Gilpin, in whose *Essay on Prints*, first published in 1769, the picturesque was defined as 'a term expressive of that peculiar kind of beauty, which is agreeable in a picture' (Gilpin, 1769 [1802]: xii). This provided Gilpin with an opportunity to suggest all manner of visual values that would enhance the appearance of the landscape, with special attention paid to texture and composition. Rough and rugged ruins, he argued, were more pleasing than architectural completeness, however elegant, to the extent that:

> ... [s]hould we wish to give it picturesque beauty, we must use the mallet instead of the chisel: we must beat down one side of it, deface the

other, and throw the mutilated members around in heaps. In short from a smooth building we must turn it into a rough ruin. No painter who had the choice of the two objects would hesitate which to choose. (Gilpin, 1792 [1808]: 7)

This fascination with the melancholy and the romance of ruins permeated the aesthetic sense of the past in Britain throughout the 19th and into the 20th century. It was coupled, too, with a delight in natural beauty and a counteracting fixation with corruption and evil, inviting an interest in ruinous abbeys, castles and graves, along with '... symbols of death and decay' (Edensor, 2005: 11). Central to this collection of representations was a desire, as Edensor (2005: 11) notes, to produce a feeling of melancholy and offer a symbolic image of '... the inevitability of life passing'. As Edensor (2005: 13) goes on to argue, this romanticization of the past was pervasive, demonstrated in the 'created' or manipulated ruins featured in many 18th and 19th century designed estates, and, as argued by Brett (1996: 43), is a pursuit that has continued to dominate today. Furthermore, the use of aquatint prints to illustrate Gilpin's other travelogues created an intense and newfound visuality and an anticipation for readers of the possibility of visiting those same monuments and landscapes as tourists – an important moment in the visual culture, and therefore the semiotics, of tourism. Layers of aesthetic meaning continued to form around the landscape and historic monuments and their ruins, including Edmund Burke's notion of the sublime (see Chapter 6) and its associations with wild nature, mythology and the epic qualities of 19th-century romanticism and antiquarianism (Brett, 1996: 51–60).

By the end of the 19th century, heritage had become enshrined in civil and professional society through the *Society of Antiquaries*, the *British Archaeological Society* and the *Society for the Preservation of Ancient Buildings* (SPAB). Eventually, it found its place in legislation, with the *Ancient Monuments Protection Act of 1882*, and the establishment of the *Royal Commission on Ancient and Historic Monuments* in 1908 (Delafons, 1997: 29). With the founding of the National Trust in 1895, and enshrined in the *National Trust Act* of 1907, the foundations were laid for a long and sustained relationship between heritage – imagined as a 'lovely view', 'old ruin' or 'everlasting delight' (Octavia Hill, cited in Reynolds, 2004: 3) – and a public newly mobile with the rail network and, later, motor transport. This public was thus equipped with the perception that, together with the hedonistic resorts of the spa and seaside, other places were *prepared* for them. These antecedents of heritage tourism provided an essentialized notion of the national past. Emblematic here are things like Stonehenge, Hadrian's Wall, Whitby Abbey and Windsor Castle. So too is the Tower of London a heritage attraction *par excellence*; a semiotic landscape with a system of representation and signification that has effects far beyond its mere depiction of the past, as Samuel's (1999) careful deconstruction of its history suggests. Here, a 'concurrence of different influences', created from a mere cabinet of curiosities, has emerged so pervasively as a monumental tourist attraction, that by the end of the 19th century it was attracting more than half a million visitors a year. During this time it began to reproduce its medievalism, as gothic revivalists, led by the architect Anthony Salvin, sought to reconstruct a romanticized gothic past (Samuel, 1999: 118).

The objects of heritage tourism need not always be so grandiose. As Cantwell (1993) has noted, it is the circulation of the body of significant representations that is important, whatever (or no matter) its provenance. This allows anything from the romance of the wilderness to 'a cardboard carton full of torpid rattlesnakes, on the lot of a gas station on a remote Nevada highway', to enter the realm of the touristic (1993: 280). These representations are, for Cantwell, the result of *ethnomimesis*, the process by which cultural material is transformed from one order of signification to another and constitutes all that is significantly represented in and about a culture. This is an essentially semiotic act, '[e]specially that unconscious mimicry', he goes on to argue, 'through which we take the deposits of a particular influence, tradition, or culture to ourselves and by which others recognize them in us'. Similarly, Edensor (2002) has catalogued the various components that are materialized and represented in popular culture in ways that effectively 'perform' national identity. These perspectives relate to Barthes' (1972) concept of myth, where a sign of something in one semiotic system shifts into another register and signifies something else, perhaps something more profound, and where the products of history are naturalized as common sense and a common identity.

Heritage thus formulates its own sign systems and significations that are historically 'proven' and which organize practices that are interwoven with concepts of national identity and the new spatialities of tourism that make it knowable and meaningful. Catherine Palmer (2005: 8) has developed precisely this point in a series of papers that explore the ways in which the past is represented through the sites of heritage tourism, selecting and excluding elements as per the dictates of a 'hegemonic discourse that [reflects] the values and agenda of those organizations that own and manage the sites'. Hers is a platform for exploring the representations of heritage tourism more specifically as vehicles for 'speaking' about Englishness, a point that holds considerable import here. This is because in using heritage to connect visitors with a core Englishness, the heritage discourse charted here is closed to contradictory interpretations and historical debate that might contest the vision as proffered, that Englishness is fixed and unchanging: *the* heritage, as Palmer so eloquently points out (2005: 9).

Though space precludes a more lavish exploration of these issues, the semiotic landscape of heritage tourism in England remains replete with such significations of timeless tradition and permanence, as any cursory glance through English Heritage or National Trust brochures will attest (Waterton, 2009, 2010a, 2013; Watson, 2013) (see Figure 3.1). Such an observation is traceable to the very convincing analyses offered by Kevin Walsh (1992; see also Smith, 2006), who has argued that the country house is perhaps most emblematic in the production of an English heritage:

> There is no doubt that it is the country house which for many people symbolizes the idea of the 'heritage' in Britain or, more specifically, England. It is this type of heritage which should be defined as state heritage, and is clearly a part of a wider hegemonic struggle on the part of the traditional conservatives to maintain their position in British society. (Walsh, 1992: 75)

At stake here is a notion of cohesive social values that serve a comfortably conservative view of the past, which was clearly replete with 'eccentric aunts', 'young bucks', 'bright young things' and servants who were 'faithful',

Figure 3.1 Castle Howard, Yorkshire. A setting for TV dramas and a well-known country house attraction (*Source:* Steve Watson)

'trustworthy' and 'diffident', images constantly reproduced and reinforced in television and cinema costume dramas.

Our interest, however, envelops the wider semiotic landscape of the heritage site in order to understand the ways in which an essentialized sense of pastness developed over time and in relation to broader social and cultural movements. Moreover, our interest lies also with unpacking the way this genealogy acts to create meaning in the present, in anticipation, *in situ* and in the thoughts and feelings taken away as experience. The particular rural-historic theme that can be detected in constructs of heritage in England, for example, *has a past in itself*, has been moulded by several centuries of accumulating meaning (Watson, 2013). The result of this process is that heritage tourism in England has garnered a particular visuality that not only expresses, but determines and limits, what is known about the past, and ultimately what is taken to be 'true' about it (Waterton, 2013).

These observations, of course, are not specific to the United Kingdom alone. Numerous studies have emerged that tackle similar analytical trajectories in a range of other geographical contexts, including Australia, Portugal, New Zealand, Denmark and the Caribbean, among others. Travlou (2002), for instance, has analysed the semiotic role of guidebooks in Athens, Greece, specifically in terms of the way they textually map only a handful of *recognizable* monuments. In so doing, Travlou argues, they reinforce the 'pre-existing mythology of the Athenian landscape', which is essentially a product of 19th century travel writing (Travlou, 2002: 110). This genealogy of Athenian heritage is resurrected in modern guidebooks to reinforce a Grecophilic place image in contrast with the qualities of the modern city (Travlou, 2002: 110–111).

A similar dynamic is at work in the heritage tourism on the Greek Island of Rhodes, where Byzantine-style churches have been marked out as places of heritage interest for tourists (Watson, 2010; Watson & Waterton, 2010a). Many of them are indicated on tourist maps and in guidebooks, and almost all of them, even those of dubious historical or architectural interest, are provided with the ubiquitous roadside brown signage. What they have in common is their architectural style and features, often small rectangular cells with apses, or larger examples based on a cruciform plan with a domed crossing, and with wall paintings, in the characteristically 'flat' Byzantine style. Early 'prototypes', such as St Nicholas at Fountoukli, provide the pattern that even recently built churches faithfully replicate, at least in the essentials; and it is the essentials, of course, that provide an active visual semiotic. The touristic significance of such churches can be directly related to their role in fashioning a Greek, as opposed to a Turkish, identity for the island. This ascription of identity was challenging given the long period of Turkish occupation and yet was made more urgent by this very same circumstance when the island was returned to Greece after the Second World War. The island's genealogy of Greek heritage was thus invoked to restore and display its identity in the post-war years, each site providing a semiotic micro-landscape of *Greekness* through the media of tourism.

Similarly, other sites that were expressive of *Greekness* rather than *Turkishness*, were selected, named, framed and elevated, to use the MacCannellian terminology. For example, the early Hellenic sites and Byzantine monastic sites, and the medieval castles of the Knights of St John who attempted to defend the island from the Turks in the early 16th century, their failure leading ultimately to the Turkish settlement. In each of these contexts, the media of tourism contribute a significant visuality to their semiotic landscape, particularly in terms of their transformation into sights for sightseers. But the point here is that this process of selection and display has been constructed by the historical trajectories of the island and its Greek identity, and by the definition offered by the contrast with its now absent Turkish culture, underlined by what has been, until recently, a neglect of Turkish heritage. It is the specific genealogy of the island's heritage, therefore, that has created expectations through the island's agencies of, and display in, the contrapuntal semiotic landscape of its heritage tourism attractions (see Figure 3.2).

Figure 3.2 Kritinia Castle, Rhodes. A castle of the Knights of St John undergoing restoration (*Source:* Steve Watson)

These explorations of heritage genealogies in England and Greece lay the foundations of the semiotic landscape that tourism then materializes as display, and realizes as experience in these places. Selby (2004, 2010: 47–48) uses the term 'stock of knowledge' to describe this combination of representations and intersubjective experiences, before going on to describe the way that meaning is constructed at cultural heritage sites:

> This knowledge has been transmitted over time by parents, teachers, religious leaders, literature, the mass media, promotional materials, guidebooks, etc. [...] No two individuals will have the same stock of knowledge. However, cultural heritage tends to encourage both the development and use of, intersubjective knowledge. From childhood history lessons to tour groups at heritage sites, place consumers are significantly influenced by others (Selby, 2010: 48).

This 'stock of knowledge' in its most developed form, tourism takes on the qualities of the imaginary, an abbreviated symbolism that represents and expresses heritage in context, in attractions and destinations, and prepares visitors for the encounter and the experience. Urry (1990) and Bruner (2005) have emphasized the significance of anticipation and its facilitation in, for example, promotional material and the paraphernalia involved in the planning of travel, although such 'pretour' narratives can be sourced in a variety of ways, each of which reflects an essentialized version or 'master story' (Bruner, 2005: 22). In reflecting the history of a place's heritage, these anticipations and representations mediate the connection between the tourist as subject and the place or places in question. The construction of such an imaginary is thus a key feature of the genealogy of heritage. The relationship of the antecedence with what is displayed, determines that which is most immediately apparent about a heritage tourism site – that which is seen.

Seeing is Believing: Heritage Attractions and Visuality

We have already indicated that visuality is a key component within the semiotic landscape of a heritage attraction and, coupled with this, we have also sought to demonstrate how we see this to be mediated through processes of selection and representation, which are themselves the result of genealogies of heritage developed historically in social and historical contexts. Thus the objects that are chosen to represent heritage – be they of England or of Greece – are projected visually through touristic agencies of display. What becomes touristic becomes visible, and the result is a sociocultural visuality indexing social and cultural significance, and stimulating further visuality in the form of interpretation, reconstruction and promotion (Watson, 2009). This process, which can be mapped against MacCannell's notion of site sacralization, is key to understanding what becomes semiotically *active* or *valid* at a particular site and even within the portfolio of heritage sites in general. In this section, we will examine more closely the components and contents of that visual realm and the modalities of display that bring it to the attention of tourists.

Our starting point will be the objects themselves, the buildings, museum objects and places to which heritage values are applied and from which touristic attraction is duly constructed. As before, we return in the first instance to some of the relatively early authorities who brought semiotics into the realm of tourism in general. For MacCannell (1973, 1976), a semiotic of attraction guides tourists towards objects that have been socially constructed for that purpose. Within this framework, tourists, as sightseers, construct a significance and 'authentic' experience in contradistinction to their modern daily lives. It is these signs of authenticity, for MacCannell at least, that tourists seek; a fact not lost on the providers of tourism who stage it for them in order to create attraction value. Authenticity thus becomes one of the key motifs; not only of contemporary tourism, but also of the way it has been studied and interpreted in the social sciences (for early contributions see Boorstin, 1961; Cantwell, 1993; Cohen, 1988; Culler, 1990; MacCannell, 1973). The original, however, is fugitive; always in retreat from the advance of the tourist in search of it. Sights are themselves constructed from objects and signs or markers that indicate their touristic significance. These markers could be interpretation boards *in situ* or off-site markers, such as maps, guide books and, nowadays, websites and social media representations (such as Google Images, History Pin, Facebook, Flickr, TripAdvisor and so forth). Markers have considerable power in constructing both meaning *in situ* and the anticipation discussed earlier. Sometimes they may even assume a significance of their own when they become the focus of touristic attention. For examples of this, MacCannell cites the empty location of the Bonnie and Clyde shoot out, and his observations of visitors at the Washington Zoo, who content themselves with the information boards at the aviary, the birds having withdrawn indoors for the winter (1999: 114–115).

MacCannell's schema provides a useful basis for understanding the ways in which the visual operates semiotically at heritage sites in marking out what is culturally significant about it. The site itself, however, often provides a semiotic impulse through the expression of monumentality created in framing and elevating it (to use MacCannell's terms). This expressed and

Signing the Past 47

perceived monumentality becomes, in itself, a marker of the site, enhancing its visuality through its physical presentation to the visitor, its excavation or tidying up, and the removal of fallen, loose or dangerous fabric; as well as the very fact of its preservation and the appearance of the measures taken to conserve it, all of which was enshrined and institutionalized, in the United Kingdom, in the *Ancient Monuments Consolidation and Amendment Act 1913* (after Schwyzer, 1999). The visual implications of monumentality are further intensified through the practices of interpretation, which may involve both text and an enhanced visuality that derives from visual reconstructions and, in extreme cases, physical ones, too. Interpretation boards can assume the significance to which MacCannell refers, as a high level of 'marker involvement'. Roman remains in Britain, for example, are often almost invisible as field monuments, but are visually 'raised' by the use of interpretation boards (Copeland, 2010).

Visuality is enhanced through the design of interpretation and its context. The ubiquitous visitor centre announces the significance of objects and places, especially where it contains exhibits of objects that have been unearthed or reconstructed, or vectored by media presentations and interactive displays. Each of these works to enclose the visuality of a place rather than open it up. It limits the number of signifiers available and stage-manages a particular version of the past. This is a process that has undoubtedly been aided by the processes of aestheticization discussed by Lash and Urry (1994), who point to the proliferation of objects that contain, not only an aesthetic component, but also an increasing degree of sign value or image 'embodied *in* material objects' (Lash & Urry, 1994: 4, emphasis in original). Thus, it is not sufficient to have a visitor centre that is informative and accurate, it must also be well-designed in a way that makes it attractive and engaging. In the field of heritage, this has meant first a kind of corporate imagery, such as that of English Heritage, the National Trust or colour-coded road signs, that announce the presence of heritage. Second, there is a focus on imagery that is abstracted from the original and embodied with symbolic value in marketing material, such as leaflets, logos and signage, and goods such as facsimiles in gift shops or other saleable items, such as children's toys (the ubiquitous pencils, rulers and erasers), pottery and jewellery, and even the type and presentation of food. Sometimes, when an object or a building itself becomes iconic, it becomes a sign of the place and of its significance. For example, the Giralda in Seville (see Figure 3.3) has become a sign of the City and as such can be viewed, ascended, purchased on a postcard or as a small souvenir statuette to take home.

On other occasions, signs become even more abstracted: a Celtic design, Anglo-Saxon knot-work, an arabesque or horse-shoe arch, a Mayan figure,

Figure 3.3 The Giralda Tower, Seville Cathedral. A monumental symbol of the city (*Source:* Steve Watson)

an Aboriginal dot-painting, a boomerang, a Chinese character, all become a little detached from their point of origin, just enough for them to be 'quoted' and referenced, but not enough for them to lose their semiotic value. Total detachment, of course, would defeat the object of the representation, and objects would be stripped of all original meaning. For example, Jones' treatment of the ornamentation at the Alhambra (Granada, Spain) in the 1850s was to create a level of abstraction that enabled him to appropriate it *as design* rather than culture. Such appropriation might, of course, be expected within the colonialism of the period. To do this, he re-invented the Moors as an essentialized other and left them behind to languish in an ahistorical netherworld (Irwin, 2004: 150–159).

More typically, such abstractions express the desired heritage genealogies of place and work at two levels that are functionally related. On the first of these levels, heritage becomes a sign of itself in the way that Barthes (1967: 41) suggests that any 'usage' or activity does in the process of becoming naturalized, or, to put it another way, rendered 'innocent' to borrow from Selby (2010: 41). So ultimately, and in a rather unchallenging and actually rather passive way, we know when heritage is near, or where it is available, because sign systems are used to indicate its benevolent, beneficial and educative presence. And however it appears, it is always presented as a 'good thing', official, trustworthy and wholesome: it will do us some good, we are lead to believe, albeit in some vague and unspecified way. As such, it may be literally signposted, it may be demarcated in a zone or a quarter of a city, it may appear in guidebooks and websites or it may be monumental, all the ways of which are described above. But what it also does, at a second level of signification, is indicate what is significant in the past of that place. Importantly, it does not indicate what is important *in* the heritage, because what is important and what is heritage are one and the same thing in this discourse. Rather, it selects from the past what is significant, and signifies it as heritage within narrative fields that involve text, visuality and spatial organization to construct a semiotic landscape around a site, a site that expresses a relevant heritage genealogy. And because it is innocent, trustworthy and beneficial, the selection that is heritage and that is semiotically constructed is accepted as equally innocent, trustworthy and beneficial. In one of the most frequently cited discussions of these processes, Culler examined the role of tourists as semioticians:

> In their most specifically touristic behaviour, however, tourists are the agents of semiotics: all over the world they are engaged in reading cities, landscapes and cultures as sign systems. (Culler, 1990: 2)

What this creates is a consensus about what is seen and worth seeing in a 'systemized knowledge of the world' and a 'shared sense of what is significant' (Culler, 1990: 4).

We will return to this later when we consider how such systemic knowledge works to create imaginaries of place. For the moment, however, we are concerned with the visual and its role in the semiotic landscape of heritage attractions, as a key form of representation. We make no sharp distinction here between the visual and other representations as others have done (Coleman & Crang, 2002: 8). Instead, for us at least, images, text narratives, personal narratives and tourist photographs are part of the same representational practice. Later we will link this broader representational continuum with non-, more-than- and other-than-representational experiences. For now, we are content to foreground our awareness that it is the visual sense that dominates both the practice of tourism, as evidenced in the notion of sightseeing, and also the study of tourism as a social phenomenon, as demonstrated by the very considerable literature devoted to it (Franklin, 2003: 82). Visuality – including the selection and ordering of that visuality – creates the modalities of display and its scopic regimes. The visual contributes significantly to the semiotic landscapes constituted in heritage tourism attractions. It is expressed in the physical and tangible presence of sites as well as the systems of signification or marking that surround and effectively realize them for touristic consumption, in everything from spatial arrangements to interpretations and marketing – the narrativizing of visual material, as Schirato and Webb (2010: 22–23) have put it.

Conclusion

Our primary purpose in this chapter has been to highlight the myriad of ways in which the visual is implicated in the semiotics of heritage. In this task we have argued that significant sites and their associated meanings caught up within the practices of heritage tourism are visualized and re-visualized, visually enhanced and scopically regimented. At the same time, we have been at pains to underscore that while this process draws attention to particular meanings, it simultaneously crowds out and negates others. Meaning, then, is both created and diminished in the acts of display. To support this claim, we have used this chapter to delineate what we consider to be the semiotic landscape of heritage tourist attractions. We have suggested that there are three motive forces at work in this landscape, all of which are underpinned by various theoretical constructs that have informed the development of heritage studies more generally. The first considered the institutional support required to support the semiotic landscape of heritage tourism. This included ideas of nationality and also that of the 'expert'. The second explored the genealogies of heritage, or the history of its development as a meaningful practice in particular places at particular times. Finally, a broad perspective of representations was introduced. This encompassed the visual, textual and the tangibility of places and objects. The more-than-representational experience was then introduced within the broad perspective of representations, but for pragmatic reasons, discussion is delayed until Chapter 5. This delineation provides a framework for understanding what we mean by a semiotic landscape and enables us to conclude, albeit cautiously, that this framework contains other dynamics or motive forces that are as yet barely understood, but which we would like at least to begin to explore.

Our movement forward from this point is to bring into play deeper explorations of the audience, the subjective and the nature of engagement. Selby (2010: 45–46) provides the rationale that underpins this movement by raising the question of more-than-representational experiences relate to visual practices. We can assume, as he does, that these processes take place simultaneously, otherwise we would have to make the case that one precedes, or is preceded, by the other, neither of which is supportable. In developing our thoughts about this dynamic, then, we also need to explore the way that semiotic agencies, agencies of display and the politics of affect mediate and modulate this dynamic in the semiotic landscape. For example, what does the visual evoke that is more-than-representational? A memory? A feeling? Discomfort? Boredom? Serenity? Something sensual, exotic? And what is intended on the part of those agencies in terms of what is evoked? Identity? Pride? Anger? Political consensus?

In addition to the momentum afforded to us by Selby's approach, there is a second dynamic at play in the unfolding of this volume, and for that we draw something from Scollon and Scollon's (2003) account of the semiotic nexus. In this, we argue, and thus have cause to rationalize, that some elements within the semiotic landscape will be more active than others. To say otherwise would be to imply that all elements act with equal force and this seems difficult to sustain. We have, therefore, to make distinctions, to identify what is 'actively semiotic' in particular places at particular times, and how these relate to heritage genealogies, representational practices and embodied experiences. This active semiotic will be revealed through analysis in the following chapters, and with reference to the three contexts delineated here.

There is also a third dynamic that is central to our attempts to push the debate forward, and we refer here to the political. This is something that is not always apparent in more-than-representational accounts (Thrift, 2004 being a notable exception) and which therefore needs to be restored to the debate, especially since it is implicated in the selection and identification of significance. We consider here Fraser MacDonald's (2002) thoughts, in light of the exclusionary practices identified by Waterton (2009, 2010a, 2013). The first and most significant effect of the expression of politics through the semiotic landscape is the definition of what is significant and, as we have previously indicated, who has the power to select places and images (and images of places) that reflect this definitional power and the interests concerned. This is based on the observation that there is a tendency for the visual, in the semiotic landscape, to reinforce a particular view of the past and, indeed, of the present. The pasts received through the genealogies of particular heritages usually pose no problem for the existing power nexus of a particular society, as they are generally products of the same processes that have come to create heritage. But there is more than this at play, as MacDonald (2002: 65–72) points out. In his case, for example, the Highlands of Scotland have witnessed, through the processes of selection associated with touristic commodification, a depletion of symbolic capital. This, for MacDonald (2002: 71), is suggestive that an over-signification of touristic space has left it naturalized and politically neutralized, so that what it claims to represent – cultural value – is but a veil for what it *actually* reflects: the intensification of competition within the tourist economy. Taking up this theme of depletion, for us, means recognizing that the active semiotics at heritage sites work simultaneously to create and diminish meaning, but to do so with purpose and agency. The semiotic landscape of heritage sites is where these processes and dynamics are at work and in flux. The cultural symbols of the past thus provide the stage and the cast of characters where meaning and power are constantly played out.

4 Marketing the Past

Any book that interrogates the semiotics of heritage tourism is compelled to deal with the rather obvious links that exist between semiotics and marketing, most often expressed through the media of advertising and branding (van Leeuwen, 2005). There is a strong historical impetus for doing so and, indeed, the clear image-centredness and connotative qualities of both have long been recognized, perhaps most famously in Roland Barthes' (1985 [1964]) essay *The Rhetoric of the Image*, where the focus for his analysis was the *intentionality* of the image's significations in such contexts. Since then, semiotics has appeared regularly in research on advertising and consumer behaviour. It is now an established method for analysing images and texts, whether drawing upon structuralist, post-structuralist or more recent philosophical underpinnings (Mick, 1986; Mick & MacQuarrie, 1996; Mick *et al.*, 2004; Ogilvie & Mizerski, 2011; Pennington & Thomsen, 2010). What we want to offer in this chapter is our own particular analysis of that relationship. For this, we draw on the particular framing of semiotics introduced in Chapter 2 and the idea of a semiotic landscape developed in Chapter 3, which allows the intentionality of the image-makers and copywriters to dissolve into meanings that are culturally embedded and dispersed through the practices of heritage tourism, felt and constituted in moments of engagement, rather than simply understood or expressed through pre-organized representational codes.

Such an approach is consonant with marketing itself, which, much broader than advertising, has developed since the 1950s as a complex of interconnected processes involving product development, customer value and marketing communications. Latterly, services marketing has been distinguished from the marketing of tangible products (Shostack, 1977), becoming a key factor in the organization of the tourism industry and broadening its scope still further. Even more recently, a new paradigm that emphasizes the production and promotion of individual experience as a source of value has come to the fore. Heritage tourism, for example, can be seen to operate as part of an 'experience economy', encompassing a broad range of activities that would conventionally be located within the service sector (Pine & Gilmore, 2011). With this in mind, the purpose of this chapter is to explore the following processes and linkages: what does marketing do in the semiotic landscape of heritage attractions? How does it modulate experience and prepare performances of, and in, place? And how does it connect with wider heritage discourses? To do so, we begin with an examination of the role of marketing narratives within broader discourses that provide a cultural context for the meanings attached to heritage, before broadening the discussion to encompass more-than-representational perspectives on the semiotics of heritage tourism.

Discourse and the Marketing Narrative

In our discussion of marketing we make a distinction between discourses and narratives. We do so in the Foucauldian tradition, with the latter giving form, expression and voice to discursive formations of power, which in turn are centred and dispersed through these processes. Within the field of heritage tourism, such narratives depend on dominant discursive elements or fundamentals to provide meaning and purpose, as well as a cultural context, for the representation of objects, sites, places, landscapes and so forth. Furthermore, they find form and substance in the representational practices associated with the preparation and presentation of those objects, sites, places and landscapes to its public. Such practices include the design of the site as both a tangible and intangible entity: a place with objects, sensed and visible, with interpretative text and imagery, the provision of ancillary services, such as catering and retailing, and the creation of the overall experience of being there (see Figure 4.1).

Marketing, of course, is closely implicated in these processes (see Ashworth & Tunbridge, 1990; Herbert, 1995; Herbert et al., 1989; Light & Prentice, 1994), more especially through the concepts of product and product development and the ways in which these are organized in order to create 'customer value' or, in touristic terms, 'attraction value'. This makes marketing, as Dicks (2000: 174) has suggested, one of the most powerful narratives in the semiotic landscape of heritage attractions, and, as such, it is closely related to other narratives that represent the materialities of the site *as heritage* and which we would expect to be voiced in the selection and interpretation of objects for display. Marketing, together with these other narratives, will then be projected onto a notional and actual audience, whose 'needs' are supposed to be addressed so that, as Neumann (2002: 41) has put it, '[...] spectacle and observer are integrated through narratives and performances that mutually energise each other'.

Figure 4.1 Visitor services at Warkworth Castle, Northumberland, UK (*Source:* Steve Watson)

The narrative role of marketing in the semiotic landscape of heritage attractions is hardly surprising given the significance of heritage to the tourism 'industry'. Indeed, the very notion of *attraction* implies the need to create products, services and experiences that hold perceived value on the part of visitors. That there should be a link between semiotics and the attributes of marketing is therefore quite obvious, and so it is a relationship that is prefigured in the very earliest attempts to understand its social dimensions. Levy (1959), for example, drew attention not only to the fact that products contain within them a symbolic as well as utilitarian value, but also to the ways that symbolic value can be captured in the emotional connections that people make with brands. This kind of symbolic value can be expressive of a variety of image attributes with which the consumer may want to be associated, especially in a period when people identify and express themselves so thoroughly in terms of what they consume, produce or do for a living (Bauman, 2001, 2007). This can be traced as far back as the writings of Veblen (2007 [1899]), and the idea that status-seeking combines with notions of identity and self-concept so as to form a basis for symbolic value in marketing.

The symbolic, then, is key to understanding the way that marketing works in terms of consumer perceptions and decision-making. With this in mind, it is easy to see how it might also work within analyses of marketing in heritage tourism, which is replete with imagery and text designed to signify pleasurable aspects of human experience and, less obviously, how it might reveal (through analysis) the cultural constructs that support its practices (Dann, 1996; Echtner, 1999; Morgan & Pritchard, 1998; Waterton, 2013). Santos (2004) employs Goffman's notion of framing to develop an analysis of ready-made frames of reference that enable tourists to make sense of what they see. We can draw here on theories that emphasize the visual to understand how the representation of things in marketing practice, and in tourism in particular, enables these pre-existing frames to connect tourism products with recognizable discourses and familiar narratives about the culture within which they are situated (Watson & Waterton, 2010a). As Morgan and Pritchard (1998: 30–31) have stated, the specific and necessarily selective modalities of tourism representation actually point to mediating frameworks of much broader symbolism in order to connect with important and familiar cultural meanings and dominant ideological concerns. Specifically, in relation to heritage tourism, these constructs take particular forms and exhibit symbolic attributes that are connected with dominant discursive elements such as identity and official or 'authorized' renderings of the past. What we have, ultimately, is an officially sanctioned version of what heritage tourism *should be like* consequently and concomitantly, a version of the past that is unequivocal though simultaneously obfuscating and selecting (Waterton, 2013: 64–65).

The point here is that in addition to site-specific and local elements, the marketing narratives of heritage sites are likely to draw upon wider narratives that shape and influence the perceptions of tourists, not only while they are there, as visitors, but also before they arrive and afterwards. This focus on the sustaining discourses and narratives of heritage tourism inevitably draws attention to the variety of textual and visual sources it employs. Initially, these have included the well-researched text and imagery that is generated within and around tourism attractions, such as advertising, guide books, brochures and postcards (Dann, 1996; Edwards, 1996; Jenkins, 2003; Mellinger, 1994; Pritchard & Morgan, 2003; Selwyn, 2010; Tilley, 2006; Travlou, 2002; Urry, 2002; Yüksel & Akgül, 2007). Echtner (1999), in a review of literature on precisely that point, observes that:

> Each researcher, as a semiotician, has attempted to uncover the structure of these tourism myths and the ritualized behaviours and encounters that they encourage or discourage. Thus, the collective contribution of this semiotic research is to expose the structure of the tourism experience as communicated by the language of tourism marketing. (Echtner, 1999: 53)

Nowadays, websites and social media would also be included, such as Facebook, Flickr, Fotki, Fotolog, Instagram, Pinterest, YouTube, to name just a few, along with, from the tourists' perspective, their own photographs as records of their experience of 'being there'. The latter significantly conjures an embodied semiotic of presence that in itself generates and organizes meaning that both reflects and refracts the representational practices associated with the 'supply side' and relates these to a concept of self. Indeed, as Selwyn has suggested in his notion of the tourist as a 'juggler in a hall of mirrors':

> ...we find advertising specialists and agencies, together with other impresarios of the tourist imagination grounding much of their image design work on the fact that there is literally no one (thus no tourist) who is unconcerned, consciously and unconsciously and on a continuing and permanent basis, with the nature of his/her self. (Selwyn, 2010: 196)

Selwyn goes on to suggest, however, that the nature of such reflections is moulded by cultural contexts and experience, which provides a link between the subjectivity of experience and the idea of discourse, narratives and the heritage genealogies discussed in the last chapter. Urry, for example, has drawn attention to the way that:

> [o]ver time, via advertising and the media, the images generated through different tourist gazes come to constitute a closed self-perpetuating system of illusions which provide tourists with the basis for selecting and evaluating potential places to visit. (Urry, 2002: 7)

For us, it is important to understand the significance of marketing practice and the performativity of individuals and collectivities in such contexts, which are in turn the products of designers, experts and service marketers as they construct the visual and symbolic realm of heritage tourism and, through it, organize and reflect the experiences of tourists.

Semiotics and the Heritage 'Product'

As was suggested earlier, the notion of product development as a marketing concept is closely linked to the concept of attraction, as a touristic value, as both are purposeful in engaging with customers/visitors and responding to their needs and wants in a way that creates perceptions of value and thereby generates revenue for the operator. A key factor in attraction value is in satisfying some need on the part of the visitor that is most often expressed in terms of leisure and recreation, and clearly heritage has been effectively 'leisure-ized' since the end of the 19th century, when it developed hand-in-hand with the emerging mobilities of tourism. Nowadays, it seems almost impossible to separate heritage from tourism, and a link with leisure and enjoyment, as well as a cultural engagement with the past, is thus implied. This is what marketeers, borrowing from Saussurian linguistics, would describe as syntagmatic and paradigmatic contexts (Cook, 2001: 66; Mick, 1986: 197). Syntagmatic meaning is created by a combination – and often sequencing – of elements and activities that generate value. Thus, syntagmatic links can be identified between heritage and leisure and, therefore, between heritage sites and leisure products, services and activities. The elements themselves become semiotically active in a sequence or combination that is, in turn, at least partly constitutive of a semiotic landscape. Heritage sites have thus become associated with certain types of leisure and manipulated to produce sequences of activity that generate value. For example, national parks imply the possibility of a wide variety of outdoor recreational pursuits and associated services and facilities. In the United Kingdom, country houses are syntagmatically linked to leisure through their aesthetics, the opportunities they provide for time spent wandering amidst beautiful and luxurious surroundings and, latterly, through the provision of ancillary leisure activities such as children's play, entertainments and speciality retailing, all of which can be included in a visit. Such visits thus become experiences where the heritage object is connotative of other activities that add value to it, and which can be designed into the experience for that purpose.

English Heritage properties, and their counterparts in Wales and Scotland, are generally ruinous medieval buildings, such as castles and monasteries, situated within well-tended grounds that provide opportunities for wandering, gazing and relaxing in the open air. More than that, they also offer opportunities for the acquisition of 'light' knowledge from interpretation focusing on what are considered interesting aspects of the site's history, performances, re-enactments, a picnic on the grass or, more simply, a 'day out' (see Figure 4.2). As a case in point, of the 400+ properties that English Heritage advertises as 'open to the public' on their website, over 240 fall under the categories of 'castles' or 'monuments and ruins'[1].

Likewise, historic villages, towns and cities signify their own qualities, such as the aesthetic of the picturesque, quaintness, tradition, eating and drinking, all of which sit alongside speciality retailing. These qualities are amply represented in the marketing of such touristic possibilities. The point is that such elements signify both each other and their combined effects in organized sequences of activity. A visit to a historic town (almost anywhere in the world where such places are marketed as such) is thus a syntagm

Figure 4.2 Wandering and gazing, Rievaulx Terrace, North Yorkshire, UK (*Source:* Steve Watson)

of elements drawn from the frames or paradigms of historical knowledge and heritage representations that are organized by cultural and ideological meaning systems.

Heritage tourism products are, therefore, signifiers of a range of activities that drive perceived value on the part of consumers, a fact that is not lost on all the planners and designers who use heritage as an anchor in regeneration projects that also include retailing, hospitality services and the 'creative industries'. Syntagmatic linkages thus become paradigmatic in the establishment of the ubiquitous cultural or heritage 'quarter', which represents a 'coming of age' for places seeking economic revival and global recognition. Semiotic landscapes in heritage can be seen, therefore, to drive value and revenue, and represent a new means for capital accumulation that creates economies with distinct spatial characteristics based on their past. There is much evidence for this, not only in the established practices of economic regeneration, but also in the centrality of heritage to contemporary tourism, as a recent report by the United Kindom's Heritage Lottery Fund has made clear:

> Heritage is the mainstay of the UK tourism economy. The breadth, beauty and cultural importance of our heritage are the most important factors behind the 10 million holiday trips made by overseas visitors to the UK each year. Four in 10 leisure visitors cite heritage as the primary

motivation for their trip to the UK – more than any other single factor. (Heritage Lottery Fund, 2010: 6)

At this level, the semiotic landscape of heritage tourism attractions is reciprocally sustaining the design of heritage products, which in turn systematically organize the resultant experiences themselves. In other words, they provide signifiers of what is considered a valid heritage tourism experience and that such an experience is being had. Marketing narratives are thus mapped into this landscape, and both define and deplete the meaning-making processes by which the past is made sense of in these new places. The marketing of such experiences will depend on pre-existing frames and culturally significant elements that are often highly visual or visually displayed, and which are organized according to an authorized discourse that signifies what the past *is*, *why* it is important and what might be validly included and, significantly, what should be left out. Once the selection has been made, its representation can be woven into marketing narratives that define product experiences that are augmented syntagmatically by other elements. These elements help sustain those experiences and may range from an ice cream van to a cafe, souvenir shops, a walk around a cultural quarter and a picnic facilitated by the thoughtful provision of suitable outdoor furniture. The point is that all of these additional elements become semiotically active in the heritage experience – validating it, sustaining it and defining it as a thing in itself.

Heritage Tourism and Marketing Narratives

This is, of course, only half the story. Marketing processes also foster the design and provision of distinctive product-experiences, and such experiences support a more-or-less singular version of the past that depletes it of any other meaning in any other terms. Marketing therefore reduces heritage to the consumption of products and services, one that is modulated by other discourses. The semiotics of heritage tourism are clear to see in the development of heritage tourism products, but the narratives of marketing point to another form of semiosis that connects these products with wider social discourses, notably through the construction of interpretative material relating to product development on one hand, and promotional material relating to marketing communications on the other. The pre-figurations of this are easy to trace and can be detected in the way that heritage became less of an elitist pre-occupation and more associated with mainstream tourism in the 19th and 20th centuries (more so the latter with its increasing mobilities). This emerging co-dependency is broadly consonant with the growing discursive value of heritage where it is related to concepts of nationhood and identity. In the United Kingdom for example, the leisurization of heritage broadened its appeal at just the time when its discursive value became most significant, a time of social and cultural fragility caused by industrialization and the fashioning of new social classes: a middle class with new power, and a working class considered in need of assimilation so as to maximize its productivity and minimize the political threat that it posed. Hobsbawm and Ranger's (1983) notion of 'invented tradition' is closely related to the same imperative.

By the end of the 20th century, the heritage industry in the United Kingdom had become almost entirely implicated in the representation of a national past that conferred identity and social cohesion, the visible symbols of which were exemplified in state pageantry, historic buildings and national collections of various sorts. On the grandest scale, it is the monarchy and the offices of Government that occupy the pinnacle of national selfhood, but the same themes can be detected at almost every level below these in the way that the past is presented and displayed. In particular, the 'rural-historic', as a particular manifestation of Smith's (2006) Authorized Heritage Discourse, has – in England at least – generated a large body of text and representational practices that evoke an idealized, bucolic tradition over the realities of rural history and the historical significance of the 'urban-industrial' (Watson, 2013). The marketing of heritage tourism naturally follows the same agenda, not least because the nation's authorized heritage discourse in its various forms provides not only the raw material for marketing heritage objects, but also a series of frames that create familiarity and recognition, rather in the way that a brand works commercially.

The brand – in this case the national brand – provides the cognitive and emotional framework within which heritage tourism can be commodified and marketed. This framework is, however, necessarily limited, as it represents an abbreviated and essentialized past. The significant issue at this stage is the level of abstraction that takes place in the process. It was argued in the last chapter that meaning in the semiotic landscape is simultaneously both constituted and depleted by the effects of discourse and the construction of narratives, and this is a point we think needs pressing further. But what interests us, specifically, is the role that marketing plays, as a specific narrative construction, and what this adds to our understandings of the semiotic landscape of heritage tourism. Crucially, it is an understanding we hope takes us beyond assumptions of a simple linear process, with powerful or commercial interests at one end, or above, and hapless tourists at the other, or below, passively consuming discourse and narrative with reckless abandon. This follows from Coleman and Crang's (2002) observation that tourists are not merely the passive recipients of carefully prepared messages that semiotically encode discourses and legitimize power, authority and identity. Rather, they point to '... the activity and performances of tourists themselves in using and manipulating images more creatively than simply as dupes' (Coleman & Crang, 2002: 8). At the heart of Coleman and Crang's proposition is an argument begun by Crang (1994) some years earlier, when he pointed out that no longer should we be satisfied with an analysis that focuses on the idea that heritage is somehow constructed prior to the experience of it, rather than *in* the experience of it. On the contrary, he proposes that not only can discourse be mediated in the emergence and construction of other narratives and in the ways those stories are apprehended and exchanged, it is also constituted *in* such moments. Top-down, one-way linearities are not required in this model of discourse and narrative. This is not to imply, however, haphazard and random discursive formations, different every time a narrative is produced. Instead, we remain mindful of the fact that narratives tend to reproduce existing discourses that are shared intersubjectively. Indeed, to conceptualize things otherwise would render the narrative either meaningless or oppositional.

Conceptualizing 'narrative' as not only the medium of discourse, but also the locus of its constant re-invention, immediately privileges narrative forms and endows them with power in the semiotic landscape of heritage tourism attractions. It also implies an emergence of meaning in the semiotic landscape, to which visitors respond and contribute. Given the pervasiveness of marketing in this environment, the narratives that are generated in support of the marketing function assume considerable significance, in their number and variety and the commensurate variety of tourist encounters with them. Marketing thus becomes one of the performances of tourism practice that reflects and refracts the context in which it is operant and to which tourists will respond either *in situ* or in making decisions about where and whether to visit. While we return to this later in considering the role of embodied semiotics in heritage tourism marketing, for the moment it is important to foreground the extent to which marketing contributes to the diverse narratives of heritage, there remaining an active agent in representing and constituting discursive formations.

Such considerations reflect theoretical perspectives that are closely related to Kristeva's (1980) concept of intertextuality and its underlying Bakhtinian concepts of carnivalism, dialogism and heteroglossia. At its most basic level, this is a concept that reminds us not to consider discourses in isolation. Rather, they ought to be seen as acting upon, and influencing, each other in a complex of subtle, dialectical relationships, with specific discourses understood in reference to other discourses, irrespective of if that reference is implicitly or explicitly made. As argued by Norman Fairclough, intertextuality thus becomes the means by which discourses are situated within (or against) a web of social, political and cultural concerns, thereby signalling the assumptions that they draw upon to underpin their position. Here, we might find an understanding of the ways in which texts that interest us in heritage tourism meet, comingle and contradict each other, and 'revitalise each other through repetition, illogical and non-exclusive opposition' (Moi, 1986: 34; see also Bakhtin, 1981). Travlou (2002: 110, 126–127) has pointed to the way that travel narratives are a form of intertextuality, where any given text is dependent on those that precede it. The result is an accumulation of preconceptions, stereotypical images and conventional clichés that crowd out alternative renderings. What Bakhtin would have referred to as an 'authoritative discourse' forms around the core cultural meanings of heritage, there allowing an authorized heritage discourse to be constantly reconstituted and recast in the narrative constructions of marketing practice.

Narratives and narrative forms are of interest because they provide points of disclosure where meaning is transacted and where, in marketing terms, a product is both defined and offered for consumption. For the transaction to be successful the product must demonstrate and offer perceived value for the consumer. In conventional terms, this will justify the exchange of a monetary price and this is, of course, often the case in heritage tourism, but it may also have to be 'affordable' within a limited time budget, such as an excursion or a day trip. This exchange of money or time, or indeed both, represents a recognition of value in the product on the part of the customer–visitor and that value is a particular formulation of meaning, the sources of which are discursively driven and narratively expressed in the semiotic landscape of heritage attractions. The complexities that exist in this landscape, not least the effects of both micro- and macro-level influences, are key to understanding the relationships and dependencies between semiotics and marketing.

The Organization of Marketing Narratives

Again, it is worth emphasising that narrative representations are not simply the artefacts of some linear formation from an over-arching ideology to passive recipient. On the contrary, such narratives are better understood as the result of complex and fluid interactions between – in the case of heritage tourism – a variety of competing and complementary imperatives. For example, there is a very clear need for objects and places to generate revenue for their owners or for those who manage a budget for them. Revenue generation is an object of marketing and may be focused on profit making or a contribution to costs, depending on the context. Revenue generation may itself be organized in a variety of ways: it might be based on a commercially driven pricing policy or it may depend more simply on voluntary donations. In each case, however, there is an implication that the price exchanged ought to reflect a value ascribed by the customer–visitor. Another imperative is likely to be the conservation or preservation of the object or place concerned, and the communication of historical and/or aesthetic value with a corresponding need for some kind of interpretation to enable this to occur. Finally, there is a need to communicate the benefits that might be linked to the experience of something different or special, or a related value such as originality, aura or authenticity.

This essentially reciprocal process is well understood in marketing. Perceived value on the part of the consumer exists and is formulated subjectively and shared to the extent that such value is widely perceived. It is also, of course, susceptible to manipulation by the producers of goods and services, whose job it is to create and communicate such value to a nominated or 'qualified' target market. It might immediately be conceded that the construction of narratives in and around heritage attractions is far from simple, that its complexities and fluidities may generate a variety of outcomes related to context and the specific conditions affecting particular sites and objects. Notwithstanding these narrative variations, the challenge for heritage attractions is always to create products with a commensurate degree of consumer–visitor attraction value, and the success of this depends on the extent to which one or more meanings can become active in the semiotic landscape. The 'active semiotic' can thus be identified easily by consumer–visitors as a demonstration of value. Product development requires clarity, along with the bundling and packaging of features and benefits, which collectively express value – most especially in terms of experiences that match or exceed expectations. The role of the active semiotic, therefore, is to represent through a clear and essentialized narrative some key meanings about the object or place that are sufficiently recognizable and familiar to generate and sustain interest.

We can return to the example of the 'rural-historic' to illustrate how an active semiotic and a distinctive cultural construct in United Kingdom heritage tourism is a particular form or facet of the authorized heritage discourse. This is because it is narrativized in a range of cultural productions that have found form in everything from the design of suburban housing to popular novels and television dramas, some of which are, in themselves, supportive of tourism. In other words, once mobilized in tourism, the 'rural historic' is narrativized in a range of promotional texts that attach its value to a range of experiences, products and destinations (Watson, 2013). In this context, the active semiotic is what narratively defines the significance of the

Marketing the Past 65

attraction and what links it to the pre-existing discourse that supplies meaning and significance.

Significantly, tension is created in the collision of meaning that is required to activate the semiotic and construct the product essence. For example, the ascribed value of the object–place will inevitably be a product of the discourse that supplies meaning and significance to such objects and places. And yet, it takes on a life of its own once it intersects with the professional practices of museum curators, attraction designers, service providers, experts, connoisseurs, educators, television producers, lay enthusiasts and other communities of interest, and especially once it intersects with the minds of consumer–visitors. The latter will carry the residues of many performances of ascribed value drawn from cultural production and representation through their lives, reinforced every time they visit an attraction, watch the History Channel, glance through tourism brochures and so forth: each will trigger their inclination or pre-disposition to re-perform that ascribed value *in situ* as a visitor.

For 'new' heritage objects and places to be effectively developed as marketable products, it is essential that they be linked through their very selection and subsequent marketing to some pre-existing narrative that they can reflect, be a part of, substantiate or provide material evidence for (Watson, 2009). Thus, 'national' stories, historical periods that are well known, easy to imagine and visualize, or which can be augmented with additional visuality through interpretation and reconstruction, provide an active semiotic that relatively easily supports the selection of a new heritage object and the product development and promotion that goes with it. These back stories need not even necessarily be 'real' history: they could be folk tales or legends, such as Dracula (Light, 2012), Robin Hood (Jones, 2010; Scott, 2012) or even a literary character (Jones, 2010). Many of these have long since entered a subjective shared 'stock of knowledge' (Selby, 2010), and have generated their own limited repertoire of signifiers. Dracula, for example, is strongly connected to the imagery of the Hammer Horror films of the 1950s and 1960s, and Robin Hood seems irredeemably connected with Errol Flynn, svelte in a green costume and 'tights', despite a plethora of other manifestations since this early film representation in the 1930s.

In terms of more substantial objects, there is a strong differentiation between archaeological or historical objects in terms of their suitability for display. On the island of Rhodes, for example and as mentioned in the previous chapter, it is those sites that materialize the island's Hellenic and medieval Christian past that are actively represented, rather than those that demonstrate its Ottoman and Turkish heritage (Watson, 2010). But it is not just the victors for whom the spoils of heritage are reserved, although such dissonance is common in heritage representations. In the United Kingdom, certain periods seem easier to represent than others and are readily supplied with the necessary signifiers. The Romans, for example, amply assisted by their visible remains, can be represented by elements of their military uniform and equipage. The Celts and Anglo-Saxons are represented by their respective sinuous knot-work designs that summon them up in an instant when used in displays, signage or promotional material. Even words like 'Celtic', Viking, medieval, Georgian and Victorian are later signifiers imposed on historical periods in order to summon meaning quickly and connect with other signifiers that mark the essentials of the period in question. But they omit a great deal more than they signify. The marketing of the past is like a traditional children's history book of familiar images and essentialisms drawn together in a linear procession from the distant past to the later and near pasts that can be evoked in marketing narratives by words such as vintage (quite old), retro (not quite old enough to be vintage, but yet stylish) and classic (of indeterminate age, but exuding quality).

The more difficult narratives to construct are those without discursive foundations. These come in a variety of manifestations, one of which is English prehistory, the period prior to the Roman invasion. This makes it mysterious and difficult to relate to in terms of a national past since it predates any existing national identities. Indeed, there is no nationally essential discourse about any of its conventional 'ages', which in any case are now held to be rather looser classifications than was once thought. Thus, the Neolithic, Bronze or Iron Ages have little contemporary cultural meaning (notwithstanding Stonehenge, of course), no clear connections with national identity and do not even provide any good stories, something that contrasts strongly with other countries and other cultures. As a result, there is a lack of semiotic activity around these periods and, with little narrative construction, the possibilities for marketing tourist access to any archaeologically significant sites are somewhat hampered. The Northumberland hill forts are a case in point, where an English Heritage-sponsored project, together with the Northumberland National Park, initiated a detailed survey and research project that yielded much valuable information (Oswald et al., 2007). The touristic ambitions were more modestly expressed, however, with the exception of a 'popular book' and some leaflets and web pages. The same could be said of other prehistoric archaeology, where only the most monumentally visible impose themselves on contemporary tourism. Prehistory is thus the province of archaeologists and a challenge to museum curators and National Park administrators in terms of creating a narrative that stimulates visits from a wider public, despite the size and archaeological significance of some of the monuments. The 'rock art' of northern Britain is another example, which, although discovered and recorded in the 19th century, has never really 'taken off' as an object of touristic interest. In short, the prehistoric in the UK is too distant and lacking in contemporary cultural significance to have attracted any kind of semiotic activity beyond schoolbook cavemen.

There are other tensions around selectivity. For example, the discursive formations around slavery and working class politics do not readily support a narrative other than one that emphasizes reform and social progress – this is the case even though there are obvious narratives that speak to the imbalances of social and political power embedded within their histories. Key figures in the process of reform are thus celebrated for their compassion and commitment to progress, rather than reflections upon a more negatively and dissonant past. Political movements are reduced to the personalities of those best known for their interventions, with philanthropists particularly prized. Historic figures such as William Wilberforce demonstrate the point. In 2007, during the bicentenary commemorations surrounding the 1807 abolition of the transatlantic slave trade, Wilberforce become the signifier of a historical moment *and* social movement, drawing attention away from the issues themselves, as well as the social and economic contexts within which they existed (see contributions to Smith *et al.*, 2011). This process of semiotic reductionism essentializes the politics and struggles of other social groups concerned, depleting their meaning.

There is something similar at work in representations of the industrial revolution and the Victorian period in general. There, however, such workings also support and make viable the idea of industrial heritage as an object of tourism. So, while the worst excesses of emerging industrial capitalism can be represented in the narrative, it is a narrative of linear social progress that predominates and sets the scene, one that is depoliticized through its focus on individuals and instances rather than social and economic contexts, causes and effects. This is particularly the case where there is any possibility of past social conflicts being linked to present day political issues. As MacDonald puts it:

> Marketing strategies frequently rely on past histories of social struggle, but paradoxically, contemporary protest is usually perceived as a threat to the meaning of the commodity, presenting unwelcome connotations of instability, disharmony and resentment. (MacDonald, 2002: 59)

According to MacDonald (2002: 59–60), this predisposition was exemplified in the way that the 'Red Clydeside' history of Glasgow was written out of its 1990 'European History of Culture' campaign.

In addition to a focus on individuals or specific events, another reductive narrative within industrial heritage discourse is one that focuses on technology and its objects, rather than the socio-economic frameworks within which they were developed. A fascination with steam-powered objects and engines of various kinds, and not least the development of the railways, is hardly matched by a fascination with the living conditions of those who serviced this technology, except within the discourse of social progress. The prominence of Josiah Wedgwood and Jesse Shirley in the heritage tourism narratives that circle Stoke-on-Trent and the various industrial history museums located in the Potteries is a good example of this. Moreover, the technology itself is represented by personalities and well-used images, such as the famous photograph of Isambard Kingdom Brunel wearing a top hat, with a cigar in his mouth. In these contexts, the politics of the Industrial Revolution, and more broadly the 19th century, are abjured in favour of claims for objectivity, supported by the work of museums and themed attractions in creating a highly abstracted narrative containing a limited range of signifiers based on personalities, individual stories and objects. Oppositional values and political movements do not form part of the industrial heritage discourse except where 'interventions' are attempted by interested groups and communities who might express a subaltern political angle. The predominant discourse, therefore, is not concerned with making links between the heritage of the industrial revolution and political conflicts, especially where these might have a bearing on contemporary political debate or affinities.

Being There

How does the embodied nature of touristic experience interact with marketing in the semiotic landscapes of heritage tourism? So far, we have considered some of the conventional semiotics of marketing in heritage tourism, specifically those concerned with representational practices. But there is also a need to respond to new ways of theorizing the engagements people have with places, engagements which appear to diminish the significance of the visual and representational, and place greater emphasis on the performative and embodied aspects of heritage tourism marketing. The implications of these for semiotic analysis are considered here. In particular, more-than-representational theories will be foregrounded, as it is these that have opened the door on a range of other ways of considering the construction of meaning in moments of engagement. Following Crouch (2010a), it is apparent that such meaning might be seen to emerge in *moments* rather than simply being drawn down from authorized discourse, however significant the latter is in organizing narrative. Tourists are, after all, 'there' and bring with them the potential for engagement with all their senses. This 'performative turn' has been, and continues to be, influential in the way that tourism practises are theorized (see Larsen and Urry, 2011 for a review of such thinking). What all of this means for what we have described as the semiotic landscape is that it becomes an even more vital and dynamic context for the creation of meaning. As Larsen and Urry have suggested:

> It is through bodies-in-motion that people perform and 'make sense' of places – physically, semiotically, and poetically. Different senses are interconnected with each other to produce sensed environments of people and objects distributed across time and space. The embodied travelling eye cannot be separated from the body that moves and touches the ground with 'performed' tourist gazes involving other sensescapes. Gazing, we have shown, is multi-sensuous. There are many tourist gazes, and one way to approach this variety is by examining the tastescapes, smellscapes, soundscapes, and touchscapes involved in performances of multiple gazes. (Larsen & Urry, 2011: 1122)

Given this positioning, the question then becomes how are these sensory perceptions organized into meaning on the part of both the producers of heritage tourism and those that consume it? From the production point of view, it seems clear that heritage tourism producers are keenly aware of the embodied state of visitors and, indeed, some of the key challenges of visitor management and product development are concerned with visitors' bodies and movement around a site, with much of the representational practice (signage, guiding, design) concerned with that movement (see Figure 4.3).

In more developed sites, such as the themed museums that began to emerge in the 1980s, the senses as well as bodily presence was engaged. Chief examples here were the introduction of sound and smell, two of the more popularly known examples of where this has occurred are at the Jorvik Viking Centre in York and the Eden Camp Modern History Theme Museum in Malton, North Yorkshire. Nowadays, the semiotic landscape of heritage tourism is likely to be characterized by an even fuller range of sensory signifiers that are designed to enhance and define the experience that is encountered in the bounded space of an attraction. This corresponds with our comments in the introduction to this chapter concerning the emergence of the 'experience economy' as an evolved form of services marketing. The Iroquois Helicopter display, situated within the Vietnam War Gallery at the Australian War Memorial, for example, introduces not only sound and light, but tactile sensations of wind too, all of which are engineered into two multimedia experiences (see Figure 4.4).

To some extent there is nothing new in this; it could be seen as an extension of the experiential dimensions long since prevalent in services marketing.

Figure 4.3 Bodies under control at Dunstanburgh Castle, Northumberland (*Source:* Steve Watson)

This is expressed in 'retail theatre', includes the various tactics employed by supermarkets and stores, from routing shoppers around the space, to accosting them with a variety of aromas and sounds (Arnould & Price, 1993; Baron *et al.*, 2001; Krishna, 2010). The signs and signifiers of movement around space, and the definition of that space as heritage-touristic with visual and other sensory signifiers, is clearly a key part of the product development aspects of marketing in this sphere, to the extent that at least some of these elements come to be expected to be *in situ* at any heritage site worth its salt. Interpretation or other information is missed when it is not provided, and becomes grounds for dissatisfaction and complaint, the standards having been set by the most innovative and interactive heritage attractions. Sites must be prepared, therefore, and must contain the appropriate elements to accommodate the bodies of visitors, the motivations and interests of whom are varied. What is significant here is that the more-than-representational aspects of the heritage experience become, through their embodied semiotics, representational and the embodied experience of heritage becomes representational of what a heritage attraction should be as a marketable product.

Figure 4.4 The Iroquois helicopter, Vietnam War Gallery, Australian War Memorial (*Source: Emma Waterton*)

In turn, the heritage attraction becomes experientially representational of what heritage is (and is not).

A final aspect of this brief discussion is the manifestation of emotions and affects at heritage tourism attractions. Again, closely following the work of Crouch, there is a strong element of emergence here. We can no longer rely on the prepared spaces of heritage tourism to simply evoke or stimulate something in the mind and body of the visitor. It may well evoke and stimulate a great deal, but not in the linear and univocal sense that might once have been conjectured. The visitor brings thought and experience, knowledge and the lack of it, affinities of various sorts, including identity with nation or social group, suitable clothing and footwear and maybe something to eat and drink. These things are impossible to examine in isolation, but from a marketing perspective there is usually much to engage not only the senses but also (and perhaps consequently) the pre-cognitive and the felt, the expressed and the inexpressible. That these are 'available' to the designers of heritage attractions is clearly recognized and appeals to sentiment, horror, affiliation, pleasurable feelings and aesthetics, all of which are likely to be registered emotionally and affectively, however difficult it is to record and measure them. The presence of others, long since recognized as important in services marketing, will also be an influence on feeling and movement, whether or not it is articulated or responded to. At some busy and iconic heritage sites, the presence and behaviour of others may indeed be one of the most noticeable elements (see Figure 4.5), as well as also operating as one of the clearest signifiers that this is what it is: a heritage tourism site. Visiting the World Trade Center site prior to the construction of the 9/11 memorial was, for example, one that relied primarily on the movement and concentration of other 'bodies' as a marker of that space, as little else, other than the presence of those bodies selling postcards and other memorabilia, was available in that regard. The body itself and the bodies of others become semiotically active (a point made by MacCannell (1976) in his discussion of the semiotic of attraction). The presence of others is also, of course, integral to the operation of the site as a marketable product and, in effect, defines it as such.

Clearly, the body and its movement through space, and the senses and the availability to the producers of marketable heritage attractions, are just as important as any text or conventional representational practice. In a way, the embodied experiences of visitors at heritage attractions and their emotional and affective registers are, and have long been, core concerns in product design and marketing. This is an idea strengthened by Nigel Thrift's

Figure 4.5 The presence of others: Crowds at the Acropolis, Athens (*Source: Steve Watson*)

(2004) and Peter Adey's (2008) theorizations of the way affective registers are engineered or built into particular social experiences. For Thrift (2004), these registers of affect may be engineered into urban experiences, while Adey (2008) explores the planning and design of affective expressions of hope, joy and so forth into the spaces of airport terminals, which he posits is an attempt to get the bodies that move through them to act and feel in certain ways. It is then easy for researchers to consider more vividly the ways in which museums and heritage sites might similarly attempt to engineer particular affective responses into their exhibitions and narratives, with bodies, in particular, being increasingly prominent considerations in those designs. The question that emerges is the extent to which these are mobilized in the service of the dominant discourses that inform narrative construction in the semiotic landscape, or whether their fluidities, the emergent qualities, evanescence and contingent nature necessarily free them from the locked-in meanings of the representational and discursively formulated. In other words, to what extent are the embodied, emotional and affective available to the marketeers and heritage product developers? To what extent are they owned by the individual visitor, experienced, knowledgeable and active? And where does the active semiotic ultimately reside? These are questions that would be well served by a framing of bodily projection in the context of remembering, by which we mean the affective memories sponsored by the spaces and places that surround us (after Connerton, 2011). This particular rendering of 'remembering' and the bodily responses it incites through interactions with museumscapes and heritage tourism experiences, will be explored in the following chapter.

Conclusion

In our field of heritage tourism, marketing is significant for two reasons: first, it creates modalities of access and engagement to make heritage places attractive for tourists; second, in practicing the first, it necessarily creates narratives that can be discovered and discourses that can be revealed. In this sense, marketing is highly active semiotically in organizing narratives that are informed and modulated by discursive regimes. As we demonstrated in the previous chapter, engagements between visitors and heritage sites are mediated by these discourses and narratives. The concern raised here is the role they play in the way that heritage sites are prepared for and consumed by visitors, made into attractions that engage their time and attention, and create an experience for which visitors are willing to exchange time and money. In terms of discourse and narrative, it seems clear that marketing contributes a great deal to the semiotic landscape of heritage sites and, indeed, that it works with other narratives, such as those concerned with aesthetics, interpretation and conservation, in order to do so. It both generates and substantiates semiotic activity, not only in terms of material and text, but also in terms of its organization and its syntagmatic relations with other activities, products and experiences.

Finally, we have elevated an issue and raised a set of questions: marketing is also implicated in the semiotics of the body and the senses, affect and the emotions. It makes them active in the semiotic landscape of heritage attractions, it makes them significant and it creates value by doing so. But how do the active semiotics of heritage tourism interact with the subjective and the personal? And how much does heritage as an emergent and situational set of meanings rely on discourse or the individual? These are questions that will be explored in the following chapters, in which heritage is more concretely laid down as constantly emergent and constituted in moments of engagement, within semiotic landscapes replete with narratives and text, and bodies that *do* things.

Note

1. See http://www.english-heritage.org.uk/daysout/properties/ (accessed 4 February 2013)

5 Remembering

A New Theory of Signification

To this point, our observations have largely revolved around building a case for understanding places and experiences connected with heritage tourism as semiotic landscapes. But, as the preceding chapters have also made clear, we intend to lay careful foundations for a new theory of signification in this volume, one that takes a fuller account of affective dimensions, too. There are two reasons for this. The first lies in the well-cited observation that heritage sites circulate with – and evoke – strong emotions and feelings that resist representation. So too by extension do their semiotic landscapes. The second emerges from the fact that 'affect', while core to the making, dissemination and reception of heritage representations, has long been neglected. The purpose of this chapter then, is to rectify this oversight by presenting a theory of signification that takes account of affect within heritage tourism, and does so by foregrounding not only our subjective interpretations of these semiotic landscapes, but their inscribing within the human body too.

In taking up this challenge, the chapter weaves together the semiotic texts and materialities introduced in Chapters 3 and 4 with the realities and responses of actual bodies caught up in their affective contagion, moving around, engaging with and interpreting the sites and experiences before them. This, for us, is perhaps our most interesting challenge, because rarely, if at all, have the concepts of 'semiotics', 'affect', 'heritage' and 'tourism' been brought together theoretically. Indeed, with the exception of the longstanding association between 'tourism' and 'semiotics', there is little consolidated work that deals with these concepts in any sort of combination. It may be that this dearth has occurred simply because they are concepts that do not work well together – but of this we are not so sure. Instead, we argue that there is considerable and convincing conceptual overlap between them: overlap that is, in fact, very productive, particularly when explored in concert with the concept of 'remembering'. Indeed, it seems to us that this might be the concept that provides the surest way of conceptually accessing and accounting for the socially produced structures of feeling that determine and shape our affective reactions to heritage sites (after Williams, 1977; see also Tolia-Kelly, 2012). This is because our abilities to respond to the semiotic landscapes that surround us emerge, in large part, from the ways in which we have already reconciled previous experiences, moments, knowledges and events. Indeed, it is through bodily remembering that our engagements with heritage spill out beyond representation, with memories *being remembered* and moving through our bodies, where they are expressed once again and come to affect ourselves, other bodies and other representations.

It is here that our 'new' semiotic theory can be read as an extension of the representational approaches we have reviewed, particularly in Chapter 2. Taking up a similar position to Caroline Scarles (2009), we pursue this extension by drawing into the mix the concepts of 'perception' and 'affordance', which collectively allow us to broaden our account and explore the ways in which representations transcend their boundaries and interact with people, often in highly designed and anticipatory ways. What we mean by this, is that a visitor's perception of any given heritage place or experience inevitably already entails responses to its representations, which will trigger a range of kinaesthetic senses and flows, that in turn act as entry points for the retrieval or (re)emergence of memories in a cycle of affective contagion. Importantly, while these particular moments occur *outside* of representational space – within sensations, feelings, atmospheres – they nonetheless unfold against or within the patterns of affordances circumscribed by their representations and materialities. Thus, our notion of contagion, which draws directly from the work of Nigel Thrift (2008), places limits on the subjectivity of perception in two clear ways. First, while as visitors we may have our own perceptions of heritage, they are formed in relation to our 'sensuous dispositions', which are culturally, economically, politically and *historically* mediated (Hayes-Conroy & Hayes-Conroy, 2010). It is here that memory – both personal and collective – comes to act as a key register, offering a sort of historical sedimentation. As a consequence, contagion does not spread freely, as not everyone will – or can – be open to the same affective transfers. Different bodies, differently imagined, will have certain affective responses already mapped onto them, defined by social expectations and structures of feeling that have built up around issues of gender, class, race and so forth (see Tolia-Kelly, 2012). Second, contagion acts at a level that lies beyond bodies too, a point especially pertinent when we think of the technological and mediatized advances characteristic of today's Western world. These, Thrift (2004: 58) argues, are being used more and more deliberately to engineer affect into a range of places, buildings and spaces, and by extension audiences, in ways that either augment or diminish their capacities to react – viscerally, consciously or unconsciously. While this can sound somewhat over deterministic, our commitment to the subjective and intersubjective remains resolute and central to our thinking.

With the above in mind, our efforts in this chapter are exerted around capturing both aspects of affective contagion, especially in relation to remembering. A key testing ground for this theorization will be that most subjective of acts, visitor photography. Here, our theory of signification will be extended to include those moments of choosing – our rhythms of intention and perception – to take a photograph, which invokes a form of sensual memory or moment of remembering, through which the past before us is lived, acted, embodied. With each shot, particular moments of our visit, along with their affections, are cut out, rendered part of our present, where they continue to be re-encountered each time those photos are viewed. As Elizabeth Edwards (2012) points out, there is something familiar in this framing that harks back to Kopytoff's (1986) biography of things, which are 'marked through successive moments of consumption across space and time' (Edwards, 2012: 222). Though these similarities are acknowledged, our intent is to push things a little closer towards those affective registers through which those moments are negotiated. Following from this, the current chapter is an attempt to open up a new line of questioning by asking what happens to us, as bodies, when we visit heritage sites: how are we changed and what is different?

Embodied Remembering

While earlier chapters worked through our understanding of the relationship between heritage tourism, semiotics and affect, we have yet to clearly articulate our thoughts when it comes to how these might merge with memory and remembering, or, using the term we adopt here, embodied remembering. These are big topics. Indeed, Memory Studies exists as an easily identifiable and multidisciplinary field in its own right, one that has been informed by an incredibly diverse array of perspectives and standpoints. These include those emerging from history, neurobiology, cognitive psychology, philosophy, literature, law, education, architecture, sociology, geography and anthropology. Here, the sorts of historicizing that might occur around the concept of 'memory' mirror, in many ways, our own discussions that unfolded in Chapter 2 around semiotics, with familiar binaries reproduced through much of the early work, subsequently replaced by post-structuralist accounts of collective representations in the later 20th century. For quite some time now, there have been concerted moves to engage with memory occurring within our own field, such that there is now no shortage of attempts within the heritage literature to draw links between heritage and memory – implicitly or explicitly (see Harrison, 2012; Macdonald, 2013; Moore & Whelan, 2007; Sather-Wagstaff, 2011; Smith, 2006; Wilson, 2013). Some of this work draws from cultural psychological traditions, with resultant analyses, like some of our own work, citing theorizations associated with the likes of James V. Wertsch (see Smith & Waterton, 2009; Waterton et al., 2010), while others have preferred to trace a more sociological tradition, drawing on familiar names such as Paul Connerton and Pierre Nora (see Harrison, 2012; Smith, 2006). Either way, 'memory' has long since been accepted as a foundational concept within the field, with heritage tourism itself understood as revolving around sites that draw heavily on the idea of memory and subsequent processes of remembering (Edensor, 1997). More than that, they are often explicitly *designed* to produce and shape spaces into those that people visit in order to make sense of, and reconnect, with various aspects of their lives. In many ways then, heritage tourism sites reflect Pierre Nora's (1989) concept of 'sites of memory', or *lieux de mémoire*, though he was not referring to such sites specifically in his own theorization. Industrial sites offer prime examples of this, illustrating the ways in which redundant sites of production can be repackaged as heritage and from there come to stand in for, and memorialize, a way of life that has since become subject to erasure (Waterton, 2011). There are, of course, many other types of memoryscapes (Edensor, 2005) that can be captured within the rubric of 'heritage' which sit alongside industrial sites, including war memorials, public commemorations, memorial sites such as Auschwitz Birkenau and Robben Island, burial sites, battlefields and more spontaneous memorials, such as those created at the perimeter of Ground Zero, Manhattan (Sather-Wagstaff, 2011). This list also includes less tangible 'sites', such as spectacles, memorial days such as Remembrance Sunday, re-enactments and other rituals for remembering the past, as well as more banal practices, such as street-naming (Hoelscher & Alderman, 2004). All of these examples are obvious candidates for inclusion within the sphere of heritage tourism, as they are places and experiences that continue to attract a large volume of visitor interest. Space precludes a more fulsome consideration of this, however, suffice it to say that the relationship between heritage and memory is a critical one.

Alongside these 'sites' there exists a broader semiotic landscape comprised of publicly available and circulating collections of signs that include postcards, guided tours, souvenirs, photographs, official accounts, brochures, websites and repertoires of narratives that support them, all of which may be mobilized in broader memory projects (see Chapter 2). Indeed, many of these have been analysed for the role they play in sustaining collective memories, especially through post-structuralist-inspired semiotic lenses, where heritage tourism attractions, *through* analyses of their semiotic landscapes, have come to be viewed as texts to be deconstructed in order to reveal implicit political messages and ideological undercurrents (see Smith, 2006; Waterton, 2013; Waterton et al., 2010; Watson, 2010). As could be expected of such post-structural approaches, the organization and deployment of power has been central to this work, particularly in those contexts where *national* memory and identity are at stake. Here, official memorials and commemorative practices, alongside a full spectrum of national monuments, landscapes and museums, have been unpacked for their implicit political meanings (see Palmer, 2005; Tolia-Kelly, 2007). As Tim Edensor (1997: 176; see also Connerton, 1989; Hoelscher & Alderman, 2004) has pointed out, in these examples, '... elites are more able to memorialize their forebears and contemporaries, while subaltern figures become marginalized', thus drawing questions of domination into the fray.

Sites of memory created at the nexus between heritage, remembering and representation are also commonly found in less official settings. Most obvious here are those attempts to mobilize materialities and experiences that resonate with messages that can be invoked in agitations *against* domination, especially those in more recent postconflict struggles over social justice, recognition and attempts to assert rights over history (Giblin, 2013; Winter, 2007). Conflict and debate over the assertion of alternative representations of the past, counter-memories perhaps, are not of course confined to those locations in which politically sanctioned violence has occurred, but are also visible in a range of localized disputes over historical memories (see French, 2012). These may be, as Curti (2008) points out, fights over representations, but they are not representations in and of themselves. Rather, as Curti (2008: 108) goes on to argue, they are 'always performed and felt between, in and through bodies and thus always work through entangled forces of emotion, affect and memory', forces that are central to the approach taken in this book. Tim Winter's (2004) explorations of the Khmer New Year Celebrations at Angkor, Cambodia, offer a useful case in point, as does Laurajane Smith's (2006) work on social memory in Castleford, West Yorkshire. Finally, we can also trace analyses that interrogate the relationship between heritage, memory and representations, to those that attempt to reveal the powerful role played by commodification processes, through which particular narratives are too easily externalized and plied to a broad array of audiences (Edensor, 1997). Prevalent among this outpouring of work is an implied separation between the individual remembering body and collective/social memory, with few attempts to meld the two. Our turn to affect is an attempt to remedy this theoretical impasse, the nuances of which are outlaid below.

Although there is a considerable breadth of literature that supports what is essentially a constitutive and recursive relationship between heritage and memory, our primary goal is to take things a step further and place at the centre of our analysis the emotional energies, auras and attachments that are also produced and performed within the process. These are what White (2006: 328) refers to as the 'experiential dimensions of memory'. To flesh out this dimension, we borrow from the field of cultural geography and emerging work there that is currently putting into play the relationship between memory and affect, with the former conceptualized as integral to notions of becoming. Primary theoreticians brought to mind here are Nigel Thrift, whose own work is indebted to that of Gilles Deleuze, Felix Guattari and Brian Massumi, who is often brought to bear on discussions of 'affect'. As discussed in Chapter 2, 'affect' is precognitive, in *excess* and socially mediated, though it coincides with corporeal immediacy (Sundén, 2010). It is here that it sees its more radical break with post-structuralism, with the body shifting beyond 'text' and 'discourse' to that of movement (Sundén, 2010: 49). Perhaps the simplest way to sum this up is to suggest that, through affect, our considerations shift away from unearthing 'truth' towards an interest in 'what things "do" to us' (Zembylas, 2006: 309). In other words, our turn to this type of theory, at a base level, simply means accepting that each heritage place, landscape, site, experience and so forth is simultaneously *two*, past and present, always in a process of becoming, through which the two eventually superimpose, but never in a fixed or entirely anticipated way (after Reynaud, 2004). Jones perhaps put it best when he remarked that:

> Memory is 'on' and working all of the time, in our bodies, our subconscious, through our emotions. It reconfigures moment by moment who we are and how we function. Memory is not just a retrieval of the past from the past, it is always a fresh, new creation where memories are retrieved into the conscious realm and something new is created in that context. (Jones, 2003: 27)

Foremost in progressing an interest in the interrelations between memory and affect has been the work of Owain Jones (2005, 2011) and Divya Tolia-Kelly (2012), both of whom have been strong advocates for conceptualizing our engagements with place as 'memorial' as much as they are temporal, performative and spatial. Perhaps one of Jones' most insightful contributions, however, has been his foregrounding of the ghostly presence of memory while simultaneously remaining mindful of the risks inherent in adopting a perspective that is too presentist. Certainly there is an emphasis on such a presentist perspective within the collective memory literature itself, given its social constructivist underpinnings (see Connerton, 1989). But there is a risk that, in prioritizing 'becoming', along with the 'inflow' of life or 'the moment', more-than-representational accounts become *too* focused on the present, devaluing the fact that, as Jones (2011: 876, citing Dodgshon, 2008: 304) argues, 'each present carry syntheses of all the past within itself at various levels of contraction'. In other words, as Bergson (1911: 24, cited in Degen & Rose, 2012: 3282; see also Anderson, 2004; Curti, 2008) has so eloquently argued, '[t]here is no perception which is not full of memories. With the immediate and present data of our senses, we mingle a thousand details out of our past experience'.

Perceptions and reactions to heritage tourism sites, and their semiotic landscapes, are fuelled, then, by reflexive relationships between emotion and memory, or bodily/embodied remembering. Bringing embodied remembering to the fore is thus a crucial way of demonstrating a break with too strong an emphasis on presentism, while also illustrating the ways in which the full range of signifying practices is put to work in everyday, sensory life. From here, the capacity to remember can be seen to intertwine with a consideration of emotion and affect, with emphasis specifically targeted at the moment in which 'the past takes on a presence *through* a representation' (Anderson, 2004: 4, original emphasis). Important here are the associated concepts of performativity, emotion and affect, each representing something of a body–social–memory experience. There are differences in approach, of course, with performativity offering a good case in point. This is a concept that some scholars, such as Bagnall (2003), Crouch (2010a) and Larsen and Urry (2011), envision *in situ*, as a feature of individual engagement, while others, such as Butler (1997), see it in social and institutional contexts. Linked with the extent to which momentary or transient (performative) encounters are constitutive in the semiotic landscape, Crouch (2002: 207) has explored the content and richness of 'embodied' encounters:

> A central feature in making an interpretation of tourism as encounter is the importance of mediation. In encountering place in tourism our bodies are important mediators of what happens and of what we comprehend to be there.

For Crouch, space is not only felt but 'apprehended imaginatively' through signs that are constructed through engagement and embodied in and through space (2002: 208). He thus points to the significance of practice, of doing in the physical co-ordinates of human relatedness. From here, we start to see that speech, movement, sensuality, imagination, as well as interaction, feeling, turning, touching and 'doing', have achieved a kind of materiality in representation that has hitherto been missing (Crouch, 2002: 209–10; see also Larsen & Urry, 2011). Here lies our debt to more-than-representational theory and the pioneering work of Thrift, which only recently has come to influence the way that heritage too, is examined, where it is enlarged beyond the scopic and moves into individual and social bodily practices so that engagement with heritage becomes *affected*. As Crouch has argued:

> [i]dentities may be constituted and characterized in practice and performativity, and negotiated with contexts. Through our bodies, we expressively perform who we are. Heritage, however it is experienced, engages in a wider self, and a wider self-other relationality. 'Doing heritage' may thus engage, amongst other things, visual representations, but it is also most likely to be considered and reflected upon in relation to other things that matter in life. (Crouch, 2010a: 63)

For us then, the role of remembering in the semiotic landscape of heritage attractions is of interest *when taken together* with the concomitant experiences of affect and emotion, and the way that these play between the subject and heritage object. In Game's (1991) account of the constructions of heritage in Yorkshire (United Kingdom), for example, the body is everywhere involved in the processes of constituting the meaning of heritage *in place*. It is thus implicated in the definition of heritage experiences through travel, and specifically, the tour. Heritage is a mass-produced memory that is paradoxically made meaningful in terms of individual experience, bodily experiences, all the senses and affect:

> ... the notion of memory as individual or personal is constantly appealed to. And it is not only memory associated with sight: sound and smell recur as the essence of the memory we are supposed to have. In short, there is an appeal to affectivity and qualitative difference of the senses. (Game, 1991: 165)

Read in such a way it would seem impossible to separate the body from the experience of place or the practices of thinking, as Ahmed and Stacey (2001) have argued. Indeed, at the most visited tourist attractions, the most obvious sensation, apart from their visuality, is the bodily presence of other tourists, getting in each other's way, getting in each other's photographs and generally having to be managed (see previous chapter). The tourist senses the presence of these familiar others all engaged in the same activity as themselves, affirming its validity in that place and confirming the status of the place as a tourist attraction. The presence or awareness of other tourists is, therefore, one of the clearest demonstrations of the dynamic interrelationship of the body, memory and the visual in the semiotic environment of heritage sites.

As Allen and Brown (2011) have pointed out, this linking of 'the bodily' with affect has extended us beyond the analytical spaces opened up by discursive/post-structuralist approaches, affording us new ways of thinking about the active process of remembering. By way of example, they use Remembrance Day commemorations to illustrate that when lived experience is no longer considered a:

> fixed enactment of a cultural code, but rather as an unfolding, embodied participation in a collective activity that does not have a single definition or mode of signification, the relation between the inert and the living, between media and people, is transformed. (Allen & Brown, 2011: 315–316)

In those moments that we are engaging in commemorative practices, perhaps during the playing of the *Last Post* on ANZAC Day, or during the two minutes of silence on Remembrance Sunday, our bodies, remembering, are subdued and silenced, rendered '... fit for commemoration' (Allen & Brown, 2011: 316). In those spaces of remembering we are provoked to act in bodily specific ways. Key to this observation is the idea that neither affect nor remembering is restricted to personal feeling alone – there is a correspondence, or contagion, between bodies and places (see Ahmed, 2004b). A child kicking around a soda can during their visit to Auschwitz Birkenau, for example, and thereby subverting the expectations of silence and bereavement, may trigger the spreading of discomfort and annoyance to those around them. These affective responses are not intentions of the memorial site itself, but rather exceed them: affect is autonomous in this regard, escaping confinement, but is simultaneously dependent upon those encounters (Curti, 2008). As Zembylas puts it:

> [a]ffect is thus understood both as a process and a product: a *process* in which one body acts upon another, and a *product* in the sense of a body's capacity to affect and be affected ... it is not just a feeling or an emotion but a *force* or *energy* that influences a body's modes of existence. (Zembylas, 2006: 309, original emphasis)

But if the body is so deeply implicated in the experience of heritage, what does it derive from and contribute to the semiotic landscapes of heritage tourism? There can be little doubt that people are affected by heritage, especially where it relates to the politics of identity and collective memory, or where passions are aroused by nationalistic sentiment or conflict with other groups (Palmer, 2005). As Rossi (2010: 88) reminds us, though admittedly she is speaking to a different context, such emotional responses align us 'with' or 'against' others. Heritage scholars have formed the concept of 'dissonance' to describe the conflictual potentialities of such heritage engagements, a concept that has obvious resonances for a theory of embodied remembering (Tunbridge & Ashworth, 1995). Tourism, as we have seen, is closely implicated in the representation of heritage, along with other forms of cultural production. Indeed, it may be the predominant mode of engagement with heritage for many people in developed societies. It seems reasonable to suppose, therefore, that there are emotional and affective engagements involved in touristic encounters with heritage and that these relate in some way to the way that heritage is signified and understood. What can this add to our conjectures about the nature of the semiotic landscape? We know that it is rich in representations, and we know that these representations evoke responses based on their visual–textual content. We also know, from Rossi (2010: 87) among others, that 'affectivity does not distinguish between representations and a "more real" reality'. Much of this might be anticipated as a result of heritage genealogies and the accretion of *a priori* meanings that the semiotic landscape of a heritage sight might further evoke, reflect or reinforce, and some of it might be contained within moments of engagement with site-specific meanings constructed in its monumentality and tangibility. What we can also add to this mix is the immediacy of more-than-representational experience, emergent, situational, subjective and embodied, but also collisions between embodied responses and expressed emotion, and between these and points of reference that are representational.

With all this in mind, the semiotic landscape becomes a place of contact between the body, felt through its senses, re-invoked through memories, re-remembering, the materialities of objects and places, the representations of these, which may be established and conventional through use, or emergent in the situation, out of which meaning emerges and re-emerges. What Crouch, in particular, enables us to do is to recast the semiotic landscape as a richer sensory environment that makes it possible to identify, *in situ*, the 'gentle politics that emerges from the quieter affects of people coming to terms with their own heritage' (Crouch, 2010a: 58). In so doing, he acknowledges the critique that has been explored in these pages that focuses on selectivity and elitism, a critique with which he 'profoundly agrees', but which he seeks to nuance and develop for a more complete understanding of such engagements. In this he acknowledges the work of other writers in the field, notably Tim Winter (2007), whose insightful analysis of tourism at Angkor Wat similarly points out the need to avoid a constrained visual perspective and take a broader view of the engagement that takes place at heritage sites, a view that includes representational factors but encompasses others, including the embodied remembering of the subject (Crouch, 2010a: 65). Clearly there is much to be gained from this new theory of signification: the nature of engagement between the subject and the semiotic landscape is opened up and the issue of visuality is effectively contextualized in the wider mélange that Crouch provides. And while other questions remain, such as the relationship between representations and more-than-representational experiences, he offers a compelling way to understand engagement, where heritage is worked and constantly reworked in contexts of performative dynamism (Crouch, 2012: 21). Further, he challenges us to explore not only the diffuse boundary between the two but the ways in which consciousness moves between them and meaning is created and recreated. In the following section, we will explore the intensities of feeling produced through visitor photography, which, it seems to us, expresses very clearly the linkages between representational and more-than-representational understandings of heritage tourism.

Remembering and Photography

Photography has been the medium and methodology of the sight-seer for 150 years. In that time, photographs have defined both the personal experience of leisure and the collective experience of place: in other words, they have resonances that are meaningful for the individual and the social at the same time. More than this, they have contributed to the meaning that places create and reproduce, which subsequently then enter the global exchange of representations that defines tourism as both an industry and subjective experience. In this process, photographs have come to affirm and validate the visual intensity of the tourist experience, something that is expressed in the very words 'sight-seeing', with the act of photography – capturing or recording a moment of engagement, an encounter with an object or place – emerging as a significant cultural act. Family or other group photographs affirm those group relationships and collectivities; but they go beyond this too, by affirming or problematizing a relationship between the photographer, place and every other representation of that place.

With all this in mind, we have chosen to delve deeper into the idea of tourist photographs and theorize them as expressing affinities other than the obvious ones associated with friends and family in a situation of leisure, informality and enjoyment. Indeed, they connect with authorized representations that are often remembered and expressed in the 'viewpoint', a preframed, readily anticipated and frequently reproduced image of an object, building or place that does homage to its cultural significance. Sometimes the image becomes iconic, in that people describe it as such. The tourist photograph is thus an important corollary of the expressive materiality of things chosen to express place, past, identity and power. To this extent, the tourist enters the active semiotic of a particular culture at a particular time, inevitably, inescapably. There is thus little that is random or accidental about the tourist photograph. Even in its intimate and familial manifestations it expresses the significance of the destinations that play host to it. The cultural work of the photograph is therefore to affirm and reinforce the materialities of social meaning: the significance of places and the past events associated with them, the relationalities of people in these places and the expression of power and permanence through culturally privileged objects.

In a recent contribution to the field, Dean MacCannell (2011: 185) makes the point that the refuge of tourist experience remains the imaginary, where, in the presence of a tourist attraction, systematic efforts are made to shut down perception and replace it with an appropriate imagery. And he goes on to assert, '... conventional tourist imagery is constructed so as to suppress all possible metaphoricity except the simple, singular and docile depiction of tourist sites' (MacCannell, 2011: 193–194). Here, MacCannell suggests that we need to pierce this image, to turn it from an image into a sign, at which point the question becomes ... a sign of what? For us, in preserving his concern with semiotics MacCannell has retained too strong an emphasis on the visual. An important challenge to this, emerging from the literature that explores the affective registers of social life, has been to take up an interest in how affect is worked through objects. Following from this, as Edwards (2012) has argued, the camera becomes an agentic object that has the capacity to elicit sensory experiences, recover memories and imbue touristic sites with meaning. This has particular resonance for the field of heritage tourism, which is today almost impossible to imagine without also drawing to mind the photographing tourist. Several recent authors have been drawn to the ubiquity of this practice, but in a way that is at pains to broaden their concerns so that the visual becomes but one expression of that practice, with the other senses contributing to an experience that may be subjective or, to varying degrees, shared or inter-subjective, and contributory to notions of affect and imagination. Bærenholdt *et al.* (2004: 69), for example, have pursued this by moving towards 'the sociality, creativity and embodiment of tourist photography', by which they mean to '... view such photography as a theatre where tourists perform various scripts, roles, technologies, relations and places to and for themselves and for a future audience'. Others, such as Jonas Larsen (2005, 2006, 2008a) and Caroline Scarles (2009, 2010), have attempted to recover these affective registers with the adoption of innovative methods. For them, more than simply granting tourists the means by which to record or document the world before them – by taking that classic postcard shot of a church, castle, canyon or temple – the camera offers a means by which to *create and take part in the world* (after Scarles, 2009: 466; see also Larsen, 2005; Urry & Larsen, 2011).

Conventional assumptions about the relationship between the photograph and memory, which have long since been theorized as attempts to preserve 'the immediacy of the moment', are thereby extended to encompass an embodied component, too. (Scarles, 2009: 474). Through this, those photographing are conceptualized as embarking upon a process of personalizing sites as they marry together their own ideological assumptions and performances with the materiality of the site (Scarles, 2009: 469). Through this process of being 'in place', individual tourists are transformed from passive viewer into active director, with the act of photographing and the resultant photographs themselves becoming co-producers in the creation and legitimization of both historical memories and conceptualizations of present-day society (see Haldrup & Larsen, 2006; see also Bærenholdt *et al.*, 2004). The process of photography, choosing to take a photograph, invokes a form of sensual memory or moment of remembering, but it is not necessarily mimetic; rather, through that process the past *becomes* – it is lived, acted, embodied, inscribing with each shot particular moments of our visit with stories along with their affections, which are cut out, rendered part of our present, where they continue to be re-encountered each time those photos are viewed.

As remarked upon in our introduction to this chapter, our theoretical case for embodied remembering will be illustrated through tourist photography. This is a practice that is characterized by a range of paradoxes: it is ubiquitous, but at the same time deeply personal; it has democratized the process of image-making, but at the same time is implicated in a limited number of scopic conventions. But, more than this, it is a practice not only rooted in social constructions of place and their shared meanings, but is expressive of moments of engagement that are performative, embodied and affective. The resultant photographs then, are not simply *taken;* they are felt and experienced, in moments in which affinities, memories, families, identities, place and even notions of what it is to be a tourist are worked through and affirmed. Thus, while 'the photograph' is, at base, a visual act, it is *made* in moments in which the visual becomes an essential factor in the production of an embodied experience. The implication here is that what we are looking at is a semiotic that extends from the visual into other senses, literally *making sense of places.*

In making this claim, our central aim is to explore how tourists' images and the practices that underpin them compare with what we might call 'official' representations of place, an authorized visual discourse, to borrow from Smith (see Chapter 3), which identifies culturally important constructs, such as national identity and a national past. These are the kinds of images we see in guidebooks, brochures, picture postcards and, latterly, official tourist websites – or the conventional semiotic landscapes of heritage tourism. In contrast to these, we position the products and processes of unofficial photographers, tourists' unofficial representations, imbued with memory, which have, up until recently, lived in albums and dusty drawers. With the internet, however, and its associated social networking sites and user-generated-content, they have a new life (van Dijck, 2008). Particularly significant here is that those processes used to be largely private. Perhaps they were shown to friends and relatives as prints or in slide shows, but with the advent of the internet there is now a new platform for unofficial images, such as the dedicated websites Flickr and Pintrest, and mapping websites such as Google, all of which facilitate the display of user-generated content. Indeed, in the case of Flickr and others, they depend on it.

To illustrate the affective qualities of the types of embodied remembering we see implicated in tourist photography, we have chosen two examples: Bamburgh in the United Kingdom, famous for its medieval castle, and Cordoba in Southern Spain, which is closely associated with Spain's Moorish heritage (see Waterton & Watson, 2012). We could have chosen almost any two places at random in order to explore our ideas, which is in itself suggestive of a level of generalizability, although we would make no immediate claims for that here. Instead, what we hope to demonstrate is that what the unofficial photographer is producing and increasingly displaying are what we might describe as three additional orders to our semiotic landscape. The *first* is 'reflective', in the sense that it seeks only to replicate existing official images, often from well-established viewpoints; the kind of photograph that Bærenholdt *et al.* (2004: 90) describe as resembling the professional 'postcard' and which therefore contributes to the 'economy of reproductions' that characterizes tourist imagery through processes of remembering. The *second* is 'affective', in which the photographer seeks to use the image to evoke feelings and memories about place and experience. Here, embodiment is key, as tourists actively, corporeally and expressively engage in the creation and framing of images in an attempt to '... arrest time and make memories' (Haldrup & Larsen, 2003: 39). In this visual order, the camera becomes a means of ascertaining understandings of the wider world, becoming, to borrow from Carolan (2008: 415), *part* of the lived body as it moves around, subsequently altering the way the site is framed and perceived. It is, then, performative.

And after all, as Edward Said pointed out, 'the very idea of representations is a theatrical one' (1995: 63). The *third* order, finally, is 'immersive', in the sense that the photographer places the 'self' or significant 'other(s)' in the frame with the object being photographed. This roughly accords with Bærenholdt *et al.*'s (2004: 105) concept of the photograph as 'memory work', reflecting a 'family gaze' where '... tourists use photography to construct memory-visions reflecting idealized family and holiday life'. In all three, embodied remembering and affect are foregrounded, with the camera itself augmenting (or not) the body's capacity to intuit which image to capture and move forward in a process of sensual remembering.

Although our interest in photographs lies beyond thinking of them as objects, our theorizing in this chapter is nonetheless based upon an assessment of tourists' own photographs. That said, their use as illustrations of our concept of embodied remembering can add, we hope, to the productive push towards a new methodological approach for 'reading' tourist photography that combines the representational with the more-than-representational (Haldrup & Larsen, 2006). The material upon which this section is based emerged from Flickr, a 'photosharing' online repository of personal photographs launched in 2004, which boasts a collection of over 3 billion images (Freeman, 2010). That number will, of course, be considerably greater now. Our review of the repository began with a brief content analysis that allowed us to count and quantify the images tourists pictured most often in relation to our selected sites – with an eye to whether they were the classic, deserted 'shots' or framed with intimations of social relationships (i.e. including people, families, couples, groups and so forth). But we also needed to flesh these images with meaning, and account in some way for the performances of both extraordinariness (the materiality of the tourism places in question) and the ordinariness of sociality (the social lives taking place), in order to allow our theorizing to capture something of affect. This has meant attending to photographs not as reflections, but as productions: we 'perform' for the camera and attempt to project our bodies in a certain way, create future memories and produce, as Haldrup and Larsen (2006: 24) point out, 'ways of being together'. The point is that we, as tourists, are aware (even if not theoretically so) that our photographs have duration. We know that they will go on to produce meanings, memories and affects long after the shutters close and do their magic. We know this because whenever a photograph is taken we realize, or presume, that there is a good chance that we (or somebody else) will look at them again and that knowledge brings with it an affective intensity. This is arguably the case even with the advent of digital photograph, as though we are now capable of taking far more photos than ever before, and can edit and delete what we take immediately, a selection of those photos inevitably seem to find their way 'off' the memory card – emerging on social networking sites, in digital memory books, in photo frames and so forth.

Bamburgh

Bamburgh Castle in Northumberland, United Kingdom, is an important heritage object not least for the purposes of tourism. There, a huge medieval castle dominates the skyline of a small coastal village, which is primarily a seaside resort with a wonderful beach, well known within the region, but not well known nationally or internationally (see Figure 5.1). If we were to return to our earlier discussions of 'official representations', which are publicly circulated within the semiotic landscape surrounding the castle, we could say with conviction that there exists a 'typical' representation. This offers a viewpoint from below, with the castle overlooking the beach at a distance, crisp outlines of turrets, doorways and defensive walls captured and reproduced. Other viewpoints are used in official representations, though less frequently, and these include shots taken from the village or from the dunes to the south. A search of the images held in Flickr using the search terms 'Bamburgh Castle' returns (at the time of writing, at least) in the vicinity of 21,000 results. Taking the first 100 images as a sample, it became apparent that 63% reproduced the same authorized viewpoint image, most of them in a fairly standard way. This corresponds with what we call the *reflective order*, which is here

Figure 5.1 Bamburgh Castle: The 'classic' view (*Source:* Steve Watson)

shaped by an authorizing and romantic representation of heritage circulated by heritage, tourism and media industries. The remaining images are divided between views from the village (see cover photo) and those from the dunes, and include self-portraits, family portraits and more jocular shots that include people 'riding' cannons and children playing hide-and-seek.

Despite some variation in the uploaded images, an initial observation is that the largest group of unofficial images reflects the 'classic', authorized view point. Our photographers are, in a sense, paying homage to the official and, to some extent, iconic visuality of the castle, which is contingently remembered, produced and expressed in their images (see Scarles, 2009). This is the visuality of medieval England, along with its permanence and power, as accompanying comments to the various uploaded images attest:

> The classic standard photographer's shot of Bamburgh Castle. You just have to do it ... don't you?
>
> The weather that afternoon (and all week) was pretty lousy. I had seen pictures of the castle and the wide beach, so I wanted to try and capture that effect.
>
> The postcard shot!
>
> One of Northumberland's most iconic scenes ...

What this view point tells us is that the 'thing' about Bamburgh is its castle, expressive and suggestive of what an authorized view of that heritage is. But many of these photographers are also engaging materially with the castle, as technologized bodies performing the 'now', through a very real engagement with the environment that surrounds them. Indeed, they are busy producing a personal representation of their visit, which they will transport home – '... to memorize, display and circulate ... to their friends and family members' (Haldrup & Larsen, 2006). These are subtly different to official representations, inflected with a personal flair, as the following comments make clear:

> Great exposure, X, and the water leads you nicely to the castle (which must be one of the most photographed castles anywhere). A nice take on a well worn classic!
>
> A very famous scene, but I like how you have worked this.
>
> This place must have been photographed thousands of times, but never like this.
>
> Fantastic clouds: I normally get sick of the Bamburgh photos but this one is spectacular.

These are certainly the simple depictions that MacCannell refers to, in which official imagery is reflected without expansion, but they also evidence our second order of unofficial visuality at Bamburgh – what we call the *affective* or *imaginative*. The movement towards taking these photos set in motion a visual, communicative act that, like spoken words, '... circulate between individuals and groups to establish and reconfirm bonds' (van Dijck, 2008: 62). We see the 'affective' primarily through the way that the castle is represented as a thing of imagination, something to be felt, rather than documented or understood, with many commentators describing the photographs as 'peaceful', 'tranquil', 'magical', 'dramatic', 'breathtaking', 'intense', 'moody', 'mysterious', 'foreboding', 'spooky' and 'evocative'. Others struggle to put into words exactly what the photos evoke, intimating a feeling, an internal response, instead. This visuality reaches back to the aesthetic of the sublime, variously imposing, daunting, mysterious, perhaps romantic or even slightly chilling, and certainly atmospheric. The use of sunsets, storms and clouds are common in these images, with visitors using the technical potentialities of image-making to achieve affects, as the following comments accompanying such photographs make clear:

> The grey and overcast sky gives this an atmospheric feel.
>
> An incredibly, otherworldly shot ...
>
> As the clouds rolled over the top of the famous castle, the colour just exploded, it made all the travelling completely worthwhile, it's an amazing experience to witness light like this after putting so much into getting there.
>
> Fantastic picture. I agree with your sentiments about 'being there' as well.

In these, the commentators are also drawing attention to the way other non-human elements work in assemblage to conjure affect – here, it is the weather, particularly, working in concert with the visuality of Bamburgh, which produces a stormy, other-worldy experience, and in so doing draws the past into the present. These images are affective, too, in that they trigger memories, with the Bamburgh landscape simultaneously existing as a representation, photographed, but as a memory and thus in the process of becoming through which the two superimpose:

> This is one of my favourite places. Some great childhood memories of a junior school trip. The people look great in it. Well taken, X, and thanks for making the memories surface.

I once had a relationship with a Geordie girl and we visited Bamburgh Castle. Loved it as much as I love this shot. Thanks for posting this one, mate.

Fantastic shot. Seem to have a lot of really bright sunsets over there. We saw a couple when we was [sic] sat in the camper at seahouses, then we went to the castle carpark and stayed there for the night. It was awesome.

Very fond memories of this part of the world ...

But what about our final order of visuality, the *immersive*? These hardly ever appear on Flickr, presumably because they are more personal, which suggests that this third order of unofficial visuality remains essentially private. Where they do emerge, we find a shared imagery of the national heritage – in the intensely visual monumentality of a medieval castle, part of the imaginative geography of English heritage, along with country houses and bucolic scenery. Our photographers recognize and respond to the authorized visual discourse that supports a selective and exclusive version of the nation's past, one for which the medieval castle is an essential and validating component. They reflect the official images in their own, they enhance them, make them expressive of what they feel about the place and *they put themselves in the picture* to make an affective link between themselves and the object. They immerse themselves. These are personal images that convey personal stories and memories. A picture postcard is no substitute, as it cannot quite connote a sense that 'we were there' other than by writing on the back of it; but, our immersive order of visuality performs this duality of roles, framing both selves and attraction within (after Haldrup & Larsen, 2003). One need only to think, for a moment, of the times one is pictured in a durable process of self-presentation performed in tandem with some form of social communication – sharing through social media real-time photos with family and friends, purposefully posed, conscious of producing an idealized memory of 'being-there'.

Cordoba

At Cordoba, we were able to detect at least some of the same features. As with Bamburgh, Cordoba has one very significant viewpoint that is often presented officially, and this is the view of the city and the Mezquita, the cathedral-mosque, from the other side of the Roman bridge – the Puente Romano. From our own observations of the photographic performances undertaken by visitors, gathered through casual ethnographic encounters in

2010, people seek out this viewpoint to take their photographs. Using the search term 'Puente Romano Cordoba' on Flickr generates close to 3000 images, many more if you broaden the search term to include those tourists who do not know or cannot remember what the bridge is called. For example, using the term 'bridge cordoba' yields a further 3694 images, with some overlap and some new images. The active semiotic, however, is within the Mezquita itself, a UNESCO world heritage site that plays out in stone a clash of cultures – the western and the oriental – within Europe (see Waterton & Watson, 2012). The characteristic horse shoe arch picked out in red and white stone, and the forest of hundreds of arches, provides in a dominant visuality an abbreviated, aesthetic of Orientalism, Islam and the Moorish period in Spain, reduced to an architectural motif (see Figure 5.2).

This is an image that is used extensively in official representations of the City, reinforced now by the recently opened visitor centre at the Madinat al-Zahra archaeological site nearby. This is strongly suggestive of Said's concept of Orientalism – a coming to terms with the otherness of oriental culture by reducing it to key terms that are reflected in the semiotics of its representation, as reflected in one Flickr viewer's comments:

Figure 5.2 Inside the Mezquita (*Source:* Emma Waterton)

Beautiful harmonious juxtaposition of the both Christian and Islamic features, coexisting peacefully, that's the essence of Cordoba, what this building is all about ... makes us wonder why we can't just all get along, regardless of beliefs, nowadays.

The search term 'Mezquita Cordoba' generates over 6000 results. Of the first 100 images provided, 49% feature specifically the characteristic horse shoe arches, especially those in the interior. Here, again, is evidence of our first order of unofficial visuality, reflecting the official representation of the site. At the centre of the Mezquita is the Christian Renaissance cathedral, which was stamped onto and into the complex after the re-conquest. When touring the Mezquita, one eventually finds oneself in the enormous domed space of the Cathedral, which generates a mere five images in the first 100 on Flickr. The active semiotic here is clearly the arch as an aesthetic shorthand for the building's Moorish past. But the camerawork of tourists is not simply a process of consumption, but produces or affords subsequent viewers a chance to re/connect:

Very special place. Thank you.

Feeling the mystery of heritage ...

Mesmerizing ... sublime.

Looking for evidence of our second order of unofficial visuality, the *affective* and *imaginative*, we can pinpoint one particular feature that appears to be significant, which is a kind of abstraction. Our photographers use light, as they do at Bamburgh, but also different angles to present the arches as a kind of abstract pattern:

The light and atmosphere are great in this shot. Well captured.

This building gave me the shivers as soon as I walked into it. It's haunting, moving, bewildering ... unforgettable.

Always an enchanting place that I will never forget.

What a beautiful space, too. I've been there a few times – it really does have an amazing, magical atmosphere.

Beautiful – almost dizzying.

An affective encounter is starkly inscribed in the comments above, which also illustrates the ways in which our engagements with heritage may be revivified, to borrow from Scarles (2009) through the act of photographing and viewing its results. These commentators, for example, are not simply viewing those photographs: they are feeling them, being transported by them, sensing them, remembering them. While the discretion to capture these images is afforded in many ways by the semiotic landscape that surrounds the site, nonetheless, they remain intentional photographs, products of choice, judgement and memory. There is a tone to the photos, an atmosphere variously labelled 'sublime', 'magical', 'atmospheric', 'dark' and so forth, that acts as a conduit for affective practices and intensities. What we mean here is that viewing the images on Flickr triggers not only reflections of previous, personal visits to this site or others like it, but a fusion of one's own experiences in the past, a consumption of the memories of others, and affects that exceed the photographs themselves. Like Bamburgh, examples of *immersive photography* are minimal, though tourists have uploaded some images of themselves or their companions, often framed by a horseshoe arch. In them, their bodies are staged, posed, as they participate in the theatrical process of tourist photography. Undoubtedly they are, in that moment, creating and inscribing on the mosque their own stories. These images are enlivened and full of life, and operate on Flickr as experiential sharing of memories that trigger memory-journeys for other travellers. As Haldrup and Larsen (2003: 40) point out, these '... memories and meanings [are] articulated through, and attached to, the image's fixed moment [but] have spatial and temporal flexibility. The single image has many stories, prompted by the viewer's multisensuous memories and travel-talk'. In these images, as a viewer, one can almost feel the realities of the visit, and see their affective contagion as visitors move around the Mezquita, engage with it, interpret it and photograph those experiences before them.

Conclusion

In this chapter we have sought to align our conceptualization of the semiotic landscape of heritage tourism more robustly with notions of memory, using the concept of embodied remembering to pinpoint the specifics of this relationship. For this, we foregrounded the subjective act of visitor photography, exploring how both the practices of photographing, along with those experiences of revisiting photographs, is an incredibly effective means by which to engage in memory work – both personally and more broadly. Much of the chapter set about working through the relationship between heritage, tourism and memory, before teasing out a clearer path for thinking through these acts of remembering within more-than-representational language. It is here that our focus on photography seemed to fit best. Hence, though we have focused primarily upon the ways in which memory and affect are woven through acts of remembering as we look across familiar photographs – triggering responses in our bodies or transporting us, imaginatively – we are also mindful that it is in those moments when we choose to take a photograph too, that we become infused with memory. In both instances, memories are brought forth and enact upon the present, but never without reference to a past.

To make this case and illustrate the affective and embodied qualities of remembering within the semiotic landscape, we explored three orders of engagement: reflective, affective and immersive. In all three, the requisite camera and associated acts of photography were understood as affording visitors the spaces within which to 'capture' their experiences and memories. Perhaps, then, the most important observation to emerge from this theorizing is that the photograph, and its making, is an interactive and embodied process of engagement and meaning-making, in which the active semiotic is disrupted in its conventional system of visual signification. The tourist photograph may begin with a simple replication of official imagery, but even at that level it is an embodied experience requiring time, effort and references to senses other than the visual. Taken a step further, it is a proactive expression of what was originally affective, of feelings evoked and a relationship with the cultural significance of the object. In a separate system of signification, tourists will immerse themselves and others in the object through the medium of the photograph, collecting embodied memories as well as experience. Revisiting these acts, as we saw in the brief case studies introduced, provoked familiarity and memory, as well as a sense of becoming, as each 'viewer's' original experience and their memories were remade, surging into view once again.

The articulations between heritage, tourism, affect and remembering that we have argued for in this chapter almost go without saying: where else, for example, do the present and past work so desperately together than in the field of heritage? That said, there is certainly a dearth of material dealing with this union in the literature, and it is for this reason that we have unpacked those articulations in a little more detail here. As well, this focus on memory plays an important role in setting up the following chapter, working particularly to remind us that even in current, everyday experiences, there are whispers of the past in play, entangled within our bodies and our relations with the contexts that surround us.

6 Living with the Past

To further develop our interest in the more personal accents of heritage tourism, this chapter foregrounds the relationships between everyday life and the places, objects and performances of heritage tourism. At essence the chapter revolves around one clear question, though it has two parts: (1) how are the qualities of places and objects understood in ways that make them significant as heritage and for tourism; and (2) how are these qualities represented in the semiotic landscapes of heritage tourism? In order to frame a response to this question, our discussions draw from the specific genealogies of heritage that bring objects and places into the representational realm of heritage tourism, and which construct imaginaries of the collective past. Of course, as we have argued in earlier chapters, not everything that constitutes heritage, or that which is deemed to *be* heritage because of some quality that is ascribed to it, will appear in the cartographies of touristic space. Nonetheless there are tangible and intangible elements at play within this context that we need to account for: objects and places, along with those intangible meanings that weave their way through traditions, identities and daily social life, as well as pervasive media representations, all impinge on the semiotic landscape of heritage tourism, working to somehow shape the engagements people have with the past.

It might be said that the entanglements between all of these 'mediate' the experience of heritage and representations of the past. To the contrary, however, in this chapter we argue that this term, 'mediate', is too simplistic, and does not necessarily lead us to how we want to think about encounters with heritage. Some of these things may of course mediate the heritage experience, but to assume that they all do – and in the same way – is difficult to substantiate. Far better, we believe, to examine the performative context of these engagements and invite speculation about what people understand from them (see Bærenholdt *et al.*, 2004; Crouch, 2010b; Edensor, 2002). Indeed, it seems to us that this sort of approach would form a most fruitful basis for future research in the area. David Crouch, to whom we have turned on numerous occasions already in this volume to help flesh out our enquiry, sums this up particularly eloquently, when suggesting that:

> [i]n experiencing a heritage 'site' we engage in a process of spacing, with its openness to possibility, disruption, complexity, vibrancy and liveliness. Heritage is constituted in being alive. Heritage is situated in the expression and poetics of spacing: apprehended as constituted in a flirtatious mode: contingent, sensual, anxious and awkward. Of course there are visual representations of heritage that are of numerous and diverse kinds. These commingle in the greater complexity of flows and heritage is thus performed. (Crouch, 2010: 62)

In order to apply Crouch's 'flirtatious mode' for our own purposes, this chapter begins by offering a discussion of the semiotics of heritage places that focuses specifically upon the way that 'place' interacts with heritage and tourism. Here, the experience of temporal depth is used as a basis for understanding the intensities of feeling that emerge in such places and spaces, as well as the ways in which semiotics, released from simple and linear object representations, enter the flows of intensity that define heritage tourism in practice and in place. Our point of inspection, though, is the quotidian because, to borrow from Urry and Larsen (2011: 1113), 'no practices escape "everydayness"'. Thus, the overall purpose of the chapter is to examine those subtler expressions and engagements with heritage that comingle with everyday experiences such as habit, memory, affective tendencies, inhabitation, movement, happenstance, skill, socializing and dialogical encounters with non-human actants too. It builds, therefore, on the notion of 'remembering' tackled in the previous chapter, in which sedimented sensibilities and embodied memories were argued to perform key roles in our *in situ* performances of openness (or not) towards the touristic experiences we encounter.

Semiotics in Place: Everyday Objects and Experiences

We seem to be surrounded by objects and images of the past, which bear down and in on us, stimulating new feelings and interacting with existing emotions, memories, thoughts and actions. Sometimes these objects and images are included in heritage representations simply to 'quote' some recognizable thought or feeling from the lexicon of such thoughts and feelings that defines a particular culture (Waterton & Watson, 2010). This particular usage may be employed, for example, in advertising or branding, to reinforce dominant discourses about places, institutions or social relations (Crouch, 2010a: 58–59). At other times, they are presented in order to evoke a specific 'something' – something emotional or affective that is culturally significant, such as identity or social coherence. Affect, then, along with its emotional consequences, is a more common feature of day-to-day experience than the literature on heritage tourism might at first suggest. It is certainly a key part of many cultural encounters. A sporting event, such as a football match between two clubs with their own unique heritage, may, for example, generate loyalty and affinity with fellow supporters, yet hostility towards those of the competing team, as well as competitive excitement that evokes intensities of feeling. Likewise, saluting the national flag may evoke deep feelings of national pride, as may the visiting of monumental and nationally recognized buildings. Similarly, those sites associated with battles, disasters and tragedies can, and often do, evoke involuntary bodily responses expressed as anger (or rage), fear (or foreboding), joy (or ecstasy). There are also things about the past embedded much more prosaically in our daily life. Here, we mean routines that evoke similar intensities and make some kind of sense in the present through meanings, associations, memories or sensual experiences, such as sight, smell or ambience. We may consider, for example, our sense of place (or placelessness) as a prosaic but nonetheless affective encounter – what makes it and what that means – and for this we can turn to Edward Relph's (1976) well known discussion *Place and Placelessness* to flesh things further. This influential publication continues to stimulate new ways of thinking about place, focusing not only on how place is *experienced*, but how it is *shaped* by the people that live in and use it. Importantly for us, Relph's phenomenological methodology drew attention to the way that places could affect and organize experience and action spatially, and in turn, the way that space could give meaning to place (Seamon & Sowers, 2008; see also Lefebvre, 1991; Massey, 2005 for various readings of this issue).

What we take from this is the understanding that spaces and places convey meanings of various kinds, and these meanings can be understood as being part of what we have called the semiotic landscape of heritage tourism. A helpful concept here is that of place-myth (Shields, 1991), by which the meanings attached to places become organized by the way they are perceived by visitors and potential visitors. As Lash and Urry put it:

> It is a characteristic of modernity that many social spaces develop which are wholly or partly dependent upon visitors; and those visitors are attracted by the place myths that surround and construct such spaces, that transform material objects into cultural objects. (Lash & Urry, 1994: 266)

Lash and Urry also make the point that while such meanings accumulate around important and culturally central locations – and here we could cite places such as London or Paris – they also develop around peripheral spaces such as the seaside (Shields, 1991). Of interest to us are the ways in which 'everydayness' and otherwise unremarked objects and places might be inscribed with significance, and the means by which this occurs. In tourism, there are very clear opportunities for this to happen through the concept of *destination image* (Garrod, 2009; Morgan & Pritchard, 1998; Pike, 2002; Selby, 2003; Sirgy & Su, 2000; Yüksel & Akgül, 2007). Indeed, it is the business of tourism, as we argued in Chapter 4, to identify characteristics of 'place' as a source of value, and while these may seem unremarkable to local people, they are very definitely grist to the mill of destination marketing. That other elusive value, 'authenticity', is often attached to such representations. In this sense places become representational of themselves and from here, archetypes and icons are likely to emerge that materialize national and local identities (Edensor, 2002: 45–48). Iconic buildings are a good case in point as they are mobilized in culture through the use of postcards and the production of souvenirs that move around the spaces that generate tourists and host them, and ultimately in the photographs that tourists take. In the tourism literature, these icons have come to be described as 'typical', yet of course what it means is 'untypical', or typical only of *this place* or *this period* and not the one it is being viewed *from*. It becomes, rather, a source of distinction or difference and, moreover, *a semiotic of that difference*. A street in an historic Spanish barrio becomes 'typical' of that city, of all such barrios, of the region in question and possibly even the country. As such, it becomes 'quotable' in touristic texts and recognizable for what it is, as a signifier. It may then be subject to further abstraction, made an essence of the thing or place to which it refers, thus finding its way into the sphere of marketing as a logo and from there makes its first appearance on postcards and as a form of souvenir. It may also be quoted in the branding of local businesses seeking to draw on its recognition and the emotional links that people have with it. Almost inevitably, it will be photographed by tourists, and often from a particular viewpoint that becomes established over time and constantly reproduced, as fleshed out in our 'semiotic orders' discussed in Chapter 5 (see Figure 6.1).

There is, however, a need to explore how things come to be treated in this way and the quality or value that makes them susceptible to such treatment. If it is axiomatic that such processes are selective, then there must be some criteria for making that selection: the selection must *mean* something and that meaning must be transformable into value in touristic terms. The role of the actively semiotic is to articulate and circulate that meaning, to connect objects not just with their representations, but with the wider

Figure 6.1 The Mezquita at Cordoba: An iconic object photographed from a well established viewpoint (*Source:* Steve Watson)

senses, feelings, emotions and affect. We might also conclude from previous chapters that such a process of selection will act on the past as it has already been made available through the genealogies of heritage, through memory and commemoration.

The question that inevitably emerges is one that tackles the nature and quality of engagements with the past in places that people occupy and visit. We may be too culturally distant from the past in western societies to understand it, other than in the texts that represent it, either through 'official history' or through the heritage and heritage tourism that both express it and deplete it. But what can be felt, especially if we acknowledge that affect not only exceeds the representational but also 'its expression or qualification in feelings or emotions [...]' (Anderson, 2006: 737). And how does this work in the context of place? In memories? What does it make people feel?

Admittedly, there is a strong academic interest in 'sense of place' that has been around for some time, matched more recently by both popular sentiment and 'official' representations within which heritage is often implicated (Hopley & Mahony, 2011; Schofield & Szymanski, 2011). But, these new versions of place, while appearing to reflect something of popular sentiment and even subaltern interest, are often aligned to corporate, partisan and authorized discourses, and simply reproduce or ignore issues of dissonance and power. This is because they often reflect and support the kind of marketing narratives referred to in Chapter 4, which seek value in local distinctiveness, the latter being a key marketing value connected to *differentiation* in product development. How else then can place be understood in relation to heritage tourism?

The Feeling of Temporal Depth

There are a range of questions that emerge from these considerations: questions about meaning and place, and the way that meaning is reproduced over periods of time through memory, commemoration and representational practice; and questions too, which interrogate the way that power is distributed through these meanings. This temporal depth is a characteristic of places that is important in national identity (Edensor, 2002: 65–66), but it also has prosaic resonances for local people and visitors as well. Feelings about places may resonate or may jar in the consciousness, and they may evoke emotion and affect in varying degrees, depending on the context and the experience of those concerned. Thus temporal depth becomes something that can be manifest in material surroundings or in the intangible realm of movement and activity (see Edensor, 2010a; Lefebvre, 2004) that contributes to the sensing and experience of place. Patterns emerge and are disrupted, lasting a while before fading away in a manner that resonates with Lefebvre's notion of 'rhythmanalysis', which Edensor describes as helping to:

> ... explore notions that places are always in a process of becoming, seething with emergent properties, but usually stabilized by regular patterns of flow that possess particular rhythmic qualities whether steady, intermittent, volatile or surging. (Edensor, 2010b: 3)

Where this dynamic patterning impinges on heritage, or where heritage is implicated in such rhythms of activity, we begin to see the myriad ways that everyday life interacts with it. There is also something reflective here of the 'ordinary affects' so deftly identified and described by Kathleen Stewart (2007: 3), the significance of which lies in '... the intensities they build and in what thoughts and feelings they make possible'. These patternings and affects enable another process of selection to act upon that which has already been determined as heritage, and begins to intimate why not every old building or place where old buildings and local traditions exist becomes a tourist destination, and why some do. The genealogies of heritage make a great deal more available than seems to be necessary for the purposes of tourism, and even the work of marketing cannot always 'add value' in ways that are comprehensible to 'qualified segments' or subgroups within the tourist population – those people with the interest, motivation or the wherewithal to visit. So to understand how certain objects come to be signified and understood as tourist attractions, a great deal more is required than their mere availability and more, we would argue, than even the representational practices associated with tourism marketing.

While we might expect heritage tourism, as a form of commodification, to be based on some form of temporal significance or depth that attracts attention, especially if it can be linked to some other significant discourse such as identity or memory, people respond to that temporal depth in various ways. They may respond to it as conventional tourists, in which case they interact with that portion of it that is an 'asset' in touristic terms, something for which they form a target market. Equally, they may respond as travellers who prefer to add to things they have discovered for themselves; or, in a similar vein, they may respond to whatever is represented to them in guide books as 'digging a little deeper' or 'off the beaten track'. Different again, they may respond as travellers who make conscious decisions to leave the tourist 'bubble' and explore the richer and riskier experiences of someone else's everyday life. In each of these instances, they – tourists, travellers, people – encounter objects and places, spaces and other people in them, all of which are busy, active and alive.

There are, as always, other sides to consider. Local people, for example, may be aware of the objects and activities of heritage tourism and weave them into their own sense of place and being, but in touristic space they may begin to take on meanings that are constructed for tourists, oddly mimicking touristic responses in a new semiotic landscape that selects and displays a commercially abbreviated account of their own reality (Mordue, 2005, 2010). Most of the time, however, local people will either not be aware of things that have touristic significance or will simply ignore them out of everyday familiarity, preferring their own more utilitarian meanings for, and uses of, the spaces in which they live and work. In this way they provide some local colour in their everyday 'authentic' behaviour, different from the tourist's everyday and therefore interesting. And, if locals are aware of the significance of touristic objects, they may still see little significance for them and may even despise that significance for the way it blocks up their footpaths, congests their traffic, raises prices in the shops and distracts their politicians. Those of us who live in historic or otherwise iconic cities (for us, York and Sydney) may be keenly aware of the crowded-meanings and 'over-signified' spaces that we occupy. Streets weave through touristic spaces and leave them again, while tourists look for significations of such changes, taking as cues the kinds of shops that are there, the cafes, the way the place looks and feels. As residents, we might walk past the largest medieval cathedral north of the Alps and barely look at it, while visitors crane their necks in amazement and find vantage points from which they point their cameras so as to 'get it all in'. And yet, as local people we know of its attraction and may well seek other similar or even lesser attractions in other places when we ourselves are doing/being tourism/tourists rather than simply living and working. Around these places of temporal depth and potential significance it is the tension, the contrast, the interplay between the quotidian and the other, home and the exotic, here and there that weighs, not only on the representations of tourism, but experiences of it. And furthermore, these are not exclusive categories. Someone's 'here' is someone else's 'there', just as someone's 'home' is someone else's 'exotic'. If semiotics is the medium through which these meanings are achieved, it is never done so in a static way: it is always dynamic, relational, contextual and emergent.

De-Differentiating Here and There

There is nothing intrinsic in an object or place that engenders touristic semiosis. Even objects that are ostensibly 'of' heritage can be ignored, overlooked and destroyed, though rates of destruction in many countries have been slowed by the onset of conservation and, indeed, the development of heritage tourism as a semiotic landscape within which tourists can perform. Rather, the process will begin with an ascription of value and meaning to an object or place that is shared to the extent that people alter their behaviour in relation to it. If this behaviour is altered sufficiently, the object becomes an attraction and the place becomes a tourist destination. The acknowledgement of this dynamic implies that while objects and places can be produced and consumed in this way, they might not always be and not always in the same way over time. A whole literature has developed around attraction formation, destination image and the idea of a 'tourism area life cycle' (TALC) that draws attention to the dynamic ways in which places are transformed into tourism and potentially out of it (Butler, 1980). The semiosis of these transformations, however, is poorly understood and has not been extensively researched beyond the managerial implications for destinations and resorts. Most studies with an interest in this topic focus on the distinction between home and away, but for us it is the interplay between the *everyday* and the *other* that expresses the touristic potential of temporal depth and which is ultimately revealed in the embodied encounters of tourists, culminating often in the moment of a photograph. In a sense, picture postcards are simply mimicking this process and indicating, with semiotic activity, the most significant objects for tourists to encounter and with which to engage with their cameras (see Chapter 5).

So, our interest is to do with the nature of 'away' and its problematic relationship with the everyday and this echoes more recent theories about how it is increasingly difficult to draw this distinction (Larsen, 2008b; see also Larsen & Urry, 2011). Indeed Larsen frames this very question in pointing out how '... the recent "performance turn" destabilizes the "tourist gaze" and highlights how many tourist practices are embodied, habitual and involve *ordinary* objects, places and practices' (Larsen, 2008b: 22, original emphasis). This is further complicated by the truncating of time and space, such that the distance that used to accompany notions of travel and tourism has become less significant than it once was, such that contact can be maintained over long distances more easily and cheaply using modern technologies (Larsen, 2008b: 24).

If tourists are less easy to define because their everyday lives are suffused with otherness in ubiquitous, easy-to-access distance-shrinking media, then their behaviour as tourists is also difficult to define because of the level of everydayness that they take with them and which dominates and organizes their practices, despite their travel and touristic intentions (Larsen & Urry, 2011): 'the self we carry with us on holiday', as Robinson (2012: 40–41) has put it. The very presence of a well-packed suitcase, in tandem with a friend, partner or extended family member, suggests that in embodied terms we are often determined to take our everyday life on holiday with us. Well-worn phrases like 'making ourselves at home', 'home from home' or a 'homely atmosphere' similarly attest to this characteristic value and contradict, as Larsen has suggested, the notion of tourism as an exoticizing experience (see also Andrews, 2005; Pons, 2003). This dissolving of tourism as a category of behaviour is thus welcome in the sense that it militates against the drawing up of taxonomies of tourist types and market segments in ways that must mean little to those who unwittingly bear such labels.

But it also implies the need to think through what tourism *does* mean in terms of performance and subjective experience. The problem with conventional concepts of tourism is that they tend to begin with an abstraction that is then applied to any number of behaviours and activities that appear to fit the bill, whether or not the 'tourists' themselves see it in the same way. Even when people 'take on' the role of tourist, they are performing something that is external to themselves and may even seek to differentiate themselves from other tourists, a tendency that began in the earliest periods of modern tourism (Thompson, 2007). Little wonder that it sits uncomfortably and jars with the everyday self they have brought with them. The surprise is not that people travel with their everyday persona and routines; rather, the surprise would be *if they did not*. That said, the question remains as to how semiotics, affect and emotion might work together in a semiotic landscape where our conventional view of tourists is disrupted by doubts about the value and validity of the term itself – doubts that are brought into sharp relief by the difficulties of separating tourists from themselves and destinations from anywhere else.

The push and pull factors associated with tourist motivations and destination image, respectively, also seem inadequate to the task of understanding these complexities. What is required instead is some theory that does not make false *a priori* distinctions between everyday 'here' and exotic 'there', and stops treating tourists as separate species. Our belief, then, is that once semiotics is released from its representational nexus and placed in a landscape of affect and emotion, where bodies interact with each other, places and objects, *then*, and only then, can heritage experiences and engagements be better understood. A corollary of this, of course, is that the notion of tourists and tourism are at once problematized and their definitional and categorical power is diminished accordingly. Tourists and tourism become mere descriptions of moments, processes, sub-processes, instances, encounters and engagements *within* a landscape that is organized around other and more significant categories that generate more powerful affective and emotional meanings: identity, memory, culture, struggle, conflict, place, mobility, visuality, performance and bodies interacting in the myriad ways they do. There are precedents, of course, for such thinking and some of these have already been touched on in this book. More-than-representational theory, for example, seems to provide a solid basis for our conjectures, although we tend towards the more-than-representational perspective. Our challenge, from here, is figuring out how the immediate and emergent performativities of tourists and tourism connect with representations, text and the visual, with a particular eye to understanding how power is distributed through these connections and how such interactions are energized and sustained.

Intensity and Indifference in Heritage Tourism

Our ruminations so far in the chapter precipitate a return to the question of significance, especially in terms of how it emerges in places in ways that alter people's perception of those places and their relationships with objects that are from – or which represent – the past in some way. This sort of thinking is reminiscent of Lefebvre's (1991) work, in which he made clear that places are not just containers of people and things; they are also active in generating meaning that reflects social and economic activity over time. In other words, they are lived in and used, and their meanings emerge accordingly. The semiotic surfaces of places are therefore uneven and variable. By extension we can infer that meaning accrues and collects around things and creates contours of intensity, often in unpredictable ways. Tourism lives in and around such intensities and imbues them with special meanings, with heritage emerging as the key element in that matrix. But what is the relationship between these meanings and others with different contours, and how are these intensities achieved?

If we return to our bigger picture of affective and emotional meaning, we can begin to see how such intensities are generated and understood. Here, it is worth considering the concept of contagion introduced in the previous chapter, in order to think through how we might frame experience in terms of emotion and affect spatially. This hooks into a number of recent theoretical debates that emphasize variation and transitions in intensity that are not solely the property of the subject, but emerge instead through the subjective experience of the body, *often among other bodies*, passing through space, being affected by and affecting spatial and temporal encounters (for an account of this in theories of affect see Anderson, 2006). To flesh this out further in the context of heritage tourism, we add Sara Ahmed's account of emotion, which she sees not as something that resides in an individual or object, but that circulates among them, sticking to one or other as they ripple and slide sideways between things, as well as backward in time, leaving traces in the present. This, she sums up most clearly in the opening paragraphs of her 2004 article, *Affective Economies*, in which she writes:

> How do emotions work to align some subjects with some others and against other others? How do emotions move between bodies? In this essay, I argue that emotions play a crucial role in the 'surfacing' of individual and collective bodies through the way in which emotions circulate between bodies and signs. Such an argument clearly challenges any assumption that emotions are a private matter, that they simply belong to individuals, or even that they come from within and *then* move outwards towards others. It suggests that emotions are not simply 'within' or 'without' but that they create the very effect of the surfaces or boundaries of bodies and worlds. (Ahmed, 2004b: 117, original emphasis; see also Ahmed, 2004a)

Ahmed's insights into our engagements with space and time act as a crucial prompt for us to think more closely about the relationship between the semiotics of heritage tourism and everyday life. If we begin by considering heritage objects *in place* for example, we might then be able to detect some of the contours of intensity that define heritage meanings among all the totality of objects, spaces and times that we encounter, inhabit and work within. In fact, we already have an empirical cartography of such meanings for any destination: all we need do is look at a guidebook or a tourist map and the points of intensity are signified as tourist attractions. The point is not, however, that they are simply attractions; rather, it is about what that attraction means and the feelings it evokes and attracts – the affect and emotion that sticks to them over time, or slides away, as people interact with them. Reflecting Stewart's 'ordinary affects', such engagements '... work not through "meanings" per se, but rather in the way that they pick up density and texture as they move through bodies, dreams, dramas, and social worldings of all kinds' (Stewart, 2007: 3). The experience of tourism is replete with such felt and negotiated meaning. It oozes in and out of objects and places making attractions as it does so; it leads us to them and away from them as we literally *feel for them* in our progress through a destination and we experience the contours of intensity around which meaning accumulates in what we have described as a semiotic landscape.

What we want to propose, therefore, is that places become intense with feeling in a way that is reciprocal with semiotic activity. This mutually modulating effect is key to understanding the ways in which the everyday interacts with heritage and heritage tourism. It influences the ways in which places become heritage tourism destinations and it invests objects with the significance required to become attractions. Examples of this are legion and span changes and developments in the way that places have been seen and felt. Perhaps the earliest examples of what we are referring to are the aesthetics of the picturesque and the sublime in the early years of sightseeing. The sublime, in particular, was a specific appeal to affect and its emotional consequences, the body in awe, apprehensive, afraid, melancholic or excited. Relatively ordinary landscapes, or at least landscapes that had previously not been *seen* as such, came to accumulate intensities of feeling that were then reflected in illustration and writing. These representations then went on to establish such feelings in the cultural nexus of the time and subsequent times. When we see and feel a landscape now, we are recalling, remembering, re-feeling intensities that were mobilized 200 years ago and which are still circulating, recast in tourism and the modalities of visitation and experience, revivified in the visualities of tourism brochures and the internet.

Ruins, and castles in particular, retain similar intensities with their representation in the 'Gothick' novel to echo and reflect a sensibility that gathered pace in the latter half of the century. Walpole's novel *Castle Otranto* and the spate of novels that followed in this genre present the medieval castle as a mysterious, menacing place full of half-light and moonbeams, a place of malaise and horror. The castle is never fully achieved descriptively, we see it only in moments and fragments, and this adds to the oppressive atmosphere, the horror and terror necessary to evoke an appropriate response in the reader's imagination (see Potter, 2005). This connection between gothic horror and the castle has been variously reinforced by touristic uses, particularly where dungeons might be employed to fire the imagination. An early motorized tourist makes the following observation on Bolton Castle in Yorkshire:

> That Dungeon has a horrible fascination for me ... The floor is wet, and in one corner there is a ring in the rock to which prisoners were chained. They tell a gruesome story of how the bones of a human arm were found in that ring when the dungeon was opened out; but one's own imagination can supply the dismal pictures without the help of facts. (Riley, 1934: 96)

While castles can hardly be described as everyday objects (although they exist within everyday worlds in some places), they do demonstrate how intensities of feeling can accumulate around a heritage object and work to activate a semiotic landscape. Cultural productions of various kinds then become vectors and amplifiers in the movement and slippage of intensities around and between objects and places. Tourism itself can be seen in this sense as a *vector of intensity*, drawing feeling and affect into and around objects and even away from them, inviting expressions of emotion. Indeed, it may use emotion in its representations in order to provoke interest and evoke affect. As such, it draws on existing genealogies of heritage to make sense of the objects encountered, and provides the means of engagement and, indeed, the terms of engagement through the semiotic landscape it constructs. These landscapes, defined by their contours of intensity, generate both meaning and experience depending on the representational dynamics that exist within them and the intensity of feeling associated with them.

Importantly for us, we see no need to imagine representational and non-representational factors as operating separately here. They may of course do so to some extent, but equally they may also be acting together, feeding off each other, mutually reinforcing and creating further intensities of feeling in and around the object. The visuality of the object may be enhanced using reconstruction or interpretation, or more commonly, some kind of interactive display; and this representational activity looks to excite or enthral the tourist with some aspect of the story that is already intense, but which is also susceptible to further intensification through representation. In this way, feelings are engaged and provoked with signs, perhaps pre-cognitively, with representations of violence, affinity, comfort or hope. Emotions may be expressed both through the representations and in response to them, and a cognitive dimension of engagement may be formed: identity, affiliation, affirmation, knowledge and so forth.

But in order to really understand how these contours of intensity are formed, we must return to our abiding concern with differences and variations in intensities and how these map onto the physical spaces of heritage tourism – such as historic cities or regions – and the experiences of people performing tourism. Taken together, these two things can help us to understand and disrupt conventional notions of both heritage and tourism. For example, the genealogies of heritage help us to understand how certain objects and places come to be invested with representational significance and emotional expressiveness. We know that the process is selective and that it provides us with ways of doing, feeling and experiencing heritage as something significant in our lives. But what is missing from the idea of heritage genealogies is the concept of intensity and how this emerges and subsides *in situ* and in subjective experience. It is in this context that intensities may work against the content of established heritage and introduce new heritages: they may suddenly appear and just as suddenly subside; they may be consonant with an authorized heritage discourse; or indeed may be oppositional to it. Yet there is a softer politics at work here, to echo Crouch (2010b), which admits a broader range of objects, stories, memories, instances and interrelationships, simply because it is not modulated by an authorized discourse, but emergent in the encounters and engagements that everyday life presents chaotically, disparately and multitudinously. Crouch (2010a: 64) has expressed this powerfully in the idea of an embodied semiotics, emphasizing the emergent quality of heritage in both place and lived experience:

> A more vital conceptualization of heritage is possible through acknowledging heritage as closely engaged in dwelling, identity and belonging. Moreover, heritage is familiarly associated with 'time': things older than our own life tend to be categorized as heritage. […] So far, we have considered how this may happen in relation to particular heritage-labelled 'sites'. Such heritage is relational amongst cultural identities, families and places. It is valuable to consider this vitalism of heritage through a particular attention to the dynamic processes through which heritage emerges at particular times, moments, durations and feelings of belonging.

In this sense, spaces, places and the meanings constructed in and around them are always dynamic, constructed and re-constructed (see Deleuze &

Guattari, 2004; Massey, 2005). If such encounters with heritage achieve a certain level of intensity they might be considered of sufficient 'interest' to achieve a level of representation – or enter MacCannell's stages of sight sacralization and touristic space, to use an existing model. With more shallow contours, they may simply be of personal, family or local interest, or remain resolutely the province of enthusiasts or professionals such as archaeologists or building conservation specialists.

In the City of York in the United Kingdom, there is a very special wall – we say 'wall', but in reality it is actually the side of a house upon which one can find an old, painted advertisement. The sign advertises 'Bile Beans', which, despite the organic sounding name, were actually a chemical concoction designed to act as a laxative (see Figure 6.2). The product is not particularly old, not at least given it is positioned within York's Roman–medieval historical timeframe, and the sign probably dates to the 1930s or 1940s. It does, however, seem to have a special place in the hearts of local people who ensure that it is repainted whenever it begins to appear weathered. On the last such occasion, the Civic Trust took responsibility for the restoration, thus introducing laxatives into the City's heritage portfolio. It is also a sign that prompts squeals of familiarity and glee from the relatives of one of us who

Figure 6.2 The Bile Beans advertisement, York, United Kingdom (*Source:* Steve Watson)

now live overseas – and these are squeals that seem to occur whenever they return to York.

It is unlikely, however, that the Bile Beans sign will ever attract more than a modicum of touristic interest; it is simply a part of the city's street furnishing that local people want to keep for sentimental reasons and because it is at least slightly older than last year's adverts. There is no doubt that this object has attracted some intensity, but applying our metaphor of contours, it remains a lesser peak in the map of such intensities for the city as a tourist destination and remains part of the everyday in its semiotic landscape.

We should remember, however, that the everyday landscape contains those very peaks of intensity that mark the city's significant heritage and heritage tourism attractions. The fact that locals and residents can walk past such intensities and either feel pride or be relatively unmoved by them – or feel both depending on the day, the occasion – demonstrates the dynamism suggested by Crouch and which we have reiterated above. The role of tourism semiotics, however, is to vector such intensities and enhance them in representational practices. The point is that heritage tourism practices are instrumental in creating encounters and engagements that evoke feeling. But while tourists are clearly the target of such practices, they might not be the only 'beneficiaries'. Some of the intensities created may interact with those already felt by residents, for example where they express pride in their city and its attractions, or in the qualities of place that owe something to objects of the past that are significant for tourism. Residents are thus encouraged to celebrate the objects and places with which they are associated, and in doing so they contribute something to the intensity that is felt by the visitor. Tourism agencies delight in the thought that residents may act as 'advocates' of the destination's qualities. Such moments transfer intensities of feeling from resident to visitor in ways that engage the visitor far more, we suggest, than text in a guidebook or brochure. Indeed, it seems to us that the human involvement in representing an object from their everyday life intensifies the intensity that is accumulated around it and then, subjectively, it slips through the experience of that object into the experience of the place, and from there affects the experience of dinner that evening, or a walk by the river, or what we remember and how.

Sometimes residents are clearly 'on board' in this way. Perhaps some of them are all of the time, while others remain hostile to visitors for reasons mentioned earlier. It could be that their relationship with the object is less intense: maybe they work there; maybe the cathedral is their employer with whom they have a contract; maybe they clean the toilets or deal with awkward tourists at the admissions desk or in the shop. The cathedral (or any other attraction or destination) is their everyday life. What this seems to suggest is that the intensities that are associated with the objects of heritage tourism are always relative to the performance of the subject, and while few social scientists would claim these days that the qualities of an object are intrinsic rather than socially constructed, we are taking a step further and claiming that they are not only constructed and represented, they are felt in different ways by different people. And, having admitted the possibility that they might be felt in different ways by residents and tourists, we might also consider how they might be felt by different groups within the resident's community and by different tourists. Opened up in this way, the contours of intensity in a given place seem almost infinitely variable, 'subjective' in the clearest sense of the word. What it also opens up, however, is the possibility – and indeed the likelihood – that some of these intensities are shared, are inter-subjective and mobile in the sense that Ahmed suggests, between object and subject and between subjective experiences. We can perhaps see now how the intensities of feeling associated with heritage tourism might swing in and out of everyday experience, reflecting what Haldrup (2009) refers to as the 'banal cosmopolitanism' of tourism, the circuits of meaning and experience that connect localized experiences with global networks of representation:

> While the turn towards performance in the tourist literature has destabilized static and fixed conceptions of places and sites it has not sufficiently grasped the networked mobilities of objects, images, texts and technologies that permit tourism performances to take place and to be represented and (re)circulated across often great distances at various sites and times. (Haldrup, 2009: 56)

The contours of intensity seen on this basis seem always to be mobile and different in different subjective experiences, and yet sometimes they are fixed and apparently immutable in circuits of cultural practice such as those evident in tourism. So while there is always the potential for such intensities to accumulate around objects, they are always provisional and measured by the extent to which potentialities are transformed into performance and practice on site and in the spheres of representation that are locally connected by global activity. Patterns of activity and intensity around objects may generate the energy they need to become represented, but there are no guarantees. The inter-subjective experience of them may generate such intensity or reflect it and, as a result, re-energize it. Intensities become represented in time, enter the semiotic landscape and enter the banal cosmopolitanism of globally circulating images and texts, captured in the representational practices of tourism managers and destination marketers and assimilated or rejected by host communities.

The cartographies of heritage seem bewildering in their variety and their negotiability, and, as well, in their relationships with subjective experience. The way that objects of heritage are used and lived in and around, and how they relate to the lives of residents and the experiences of tourists, are clearly complex and variable. But the kinds of intensities we have described can accumulate around some objects and we can see how this might happen within the context of the genealogies of heritage and the imaginaries that develop around places and pasts. We can also understand how and why such intensities do not develop around certain objects. It is apparent, for example, that not every object of archaeological significance, for example, accumulates the kinds of intensity of feeling around it that are recognizable in the case of the Bile Beans sign. Objects seem to exist without being marked, signified or felt in any way and make not the slightest undulation in the contours of intensity that influence the way a place is used, understood or visited.

Conclusion

We might return by way of explanation to the genealogies of heritage mentioned in earlier chapters. Objects with no story or place in other stories are quite common among the objects of the past, and if we regard heritage as a social and cultural process separate from the objects to which it refers, we might even claim that such objects had not yet entered the sphere of heritage at all, but remained resolutely archaeological (Watson, 2009). Much of the archaeology of the United Kingdom is of this sort, invisible and disregarded, and yet the same can be said of standing archaeology in other countries where there is no tradition of building conservation and the associated sentiment around the need for such conservation (Abu-Khafajah, 2010). Prehistoric monuments and many Roman sites in the United Kingdom tend to be treated in this way, largely because of their invisibility in the landscape (Copeland, 2010), although, even where they are monumental in character, if they are difficult to fit with national stories they tend to be ignored for the most part: uninherited heritage, they might be termed (Grydehøj, 2010). Such intensities that do accumulate around them have been recent and facilitated by the additional potentialities of the internet in creating communities of interest and circuits of representation that are not dependent on local activity but which can operate remotely. Websites, such as The Megalithic Portal, work to create such circuits and intensities, and in time may change the way such objects are regarded, both by local residents and potential visitors.

What this all amounts to is this: official versions of the past, personal experience, memory, living, being in a place, visiting for the first time and revisiting are all performances of the past that influence and impinge on the ways that heritage is experienced through the global vectors that tourism represents. It is clear, however, that the labelled, officially signified and marketed heritage of the 'toured' world is highly contingent, not only in its socially constructed frameworks, but in the affective and emotional worlds of those who live with it and those who visit. Such flows and dynamics, as can be detected and which have formed the focus of this discussion, are difficult to encapsulate theoretically and harder still to imagine in their seemingly infinite variety. In this chapter then, we have sought to loosen the grip of the representational in depicting heritage tourism as a linear system of meanings made and found around objects. In acknowledging our debt to theorists such as David Crouch, we have explored new relationships between the everyday, tourism and heritage, and in so doing we hope that we have contributed to the debate around the ontologies of these categories of individual and shared experience. Finally, we have proposed a new role for semiotics in this context: released from its objects, it joins the flows of intensity that marks significance and enhances them, and fills the spaces between representational and performative dynamics.

7 Conclusions

In drawing together the various strands of thought that have formed our discussions in this volume, we have an opportunity to take stock while also mapping out how these might advance debate in terms of ideas and underpinning research. In planning this book, we were conscious that developments around representational and non-representational theory had left the former rather hanging in the air, awaiting some resolution about its future use and relationship with what we have termed emerging more-than-representational approaches. This is nowhere more important (or apparent) than in the analyses of semiotics and discourse, both of which have been mobilized in theorizations in the fields of heritage and tourism over the last few decades, though they have been applied to heritage tourism specifically relatively infrequently. It was with this in mind that we framed the volume's overarching analysis, envisioning a semiotic landscape that contains and conditions semiotic activity of all kinds in and around a heritage site, a nexus in which meaning is not only made but dynamically remade, constituted, repeated, structured and found. Having undertaken a largely theoretical journey informed by emerging theorizations, we therefore begin our conclusions with some thoughts about where it has taken us, particularly in terms of conventional semiotic analyses of heritage tourism. We then examine the implications of this for a critical review of heritage tourism itself. Finally, we draw the volume to a close by proposing an expanded, and certainly 'embodied', semiotics as the principal means for studying touristic encounters with heritage. Throughout the conclusion, we also tease out and reflect upon some of the implications this approach has for research practices. We are also keenly aware that our analysis is positioned within a burgeoning literature that is amply demonstrated within the series of books to which this one is another contribution. Being a part of such momentum is a satisfying way to conclude our thoughts.

A New Semiotics of Heritage Tourism

The association of semiotics with structuralist and post-structuralist representational theory has been problematic since the emergence of concerns with the situational, emergent, embodied and performative aspects of engagement with place and space. The centrality of text and other cultural products as vectors of meaning, ciphers through which the very nature of society – its structure, identity politics and its power relations – can be revealed, effectively filled out the space for academic inquiry. In heritage tourism, it culminated in the application of discourse analysis to the myriad texts and images through which it was represented, and which were eagerly interrogated by researchers armed with important new theoretical constructs, such as Smith's (2006) Authorized Heritage Discourse, its antecedents and its variants. There can be no doubt that these applications have, and continue to offer, compelling insights into the way that heritage and heritage tourism carry meaning and do 'cultural work', especially in relation to identity and belonging, and are mobilized, particularly, whenever these are threatened.

A panoply of other cultural forms and practices falls into place behind such representations, there working to legitimize and sustain them. Aesthetics, archaeology, art history, museums and curatorship engender an expertise, connoisseurship and professionalism that empower the ascription of significance and the selection of objects for representation and, by consequence, limit that power to qualified individuals and groups. Inevitably such power is aligned to its distribution in society as a whole and enlisted in the reproduction of identity and social structure, which are then displayed in other cultural productions such as the media, entertainments of various kinds and, not least, heritage tourism itself. In each of these practices, sign systems are used to create and sustain meaning, but also, as well we know, to limit and deplete it. The semiotic landscapes of heritage attractions are where these signs are active in representing the past in the present, there making sense of the social world as it is, with appropriate antecedents, evocations, values and legitimations. Heritage attractions are rich with such signs, but limited in terms of their overall meaning, depleted of everything but the official, the sanctioned or the commercially viable – with these usually amounting to the same thing in any case. The active semiotics around heritage sites thus create meanings that are exclusive of other renderings and which are supported in their privileged position through reference to the professional expertise mentioned above and the creation of specialist knowledge.

In the semiotic landscape, signs are traded for experiences, but at this point we would have to recognize that the representational theories that are so useful in elucidating the cultural work of heritage objects have reached their own limitations – and it is the issue of experience that lies at the heart of this problem. The turn to performativity, affect and practice in the social sciences – captured by the more-than-representational as these concepts as a collective are often called – disrupts the gaze that encapsulates the representational domain, and asks questions that it cannot answer. So now we are concerned with encounters and engagements, moments of subjective and emergent meaning making, and we are faced with a choice about whether to abandon the representational for the new dimensions offered by more-than-representational theories.

In response, we have argued in this book that such drastic measures are not only unnecessary, but also risk losing the considerable value of the contribution made by representational theory in understanding the social world. For our part then, situated as we are within the sphere of heritage tourism, we offer not a compromise but an understanding of the *potential* of more-than-representational perspectives in advancing theory. With this in mind we seek a new approach to semiotics, one that does not take us *beyond* the representational so much as *renewing* it, pushing it into the realm of lived experience, which is mobilized in the encounters, engagements, performances and practices that characterize not only tourism but everyday life. In so doing, we accept that the 'day-to-day' and the 'touristic' are less oppositional than has been conventionally thought. Instead, we argue that what marks places and objects are the intensities of affect and emotion that are, following Kathleen Stewart and David Crouch, created relationally, which is to say in the relation between the object and the subjective imagination. Here, the semiotic landscape is experienced evanescently in moments of engagement when heritage tourism is made meaningful. It is felt in the contours of intensity that mark significant places, intensities that are felt subjectively and inter-subjectively, and which are represented or simply experienced bodily or emotionally.

None of this precludes the importance of representations, textual and visual. Our position, rather, is that all of these things are implicated in the construction of experience; it is simply that they do not exist on their own. They are but elements, albeit important ones, in broader semiotic landscapes of heritage tourism. Tourism itself vectors those representations reciprocally with feelings of intensity and expressions of emotion. Sometimes these are captured in representations in order to stimulate feeling and spread it, and the intensity, being fluid, will move between people and objects: this is a contagion that defines experience, place and engagement; it is also a contagion that creates and reproduces meanings, including those that are patterned into the representational practices that produce, for example, the national past, the landscape, the familiar, the exotic and the toured.

The Implications for Critical Studies in Heritage Tourism

Of course it is not enough to understand where we are theoretically. We must also understand where all of this takes us in terms of developing what we have elsewhere called a 'critical imagination' in heritage studies (Waterton & Watson, 2013). In this, we argue for the capacity to deconstruct not only text, but also experience, where this is formed in the semiotic landscapes of heritage tourism. Implicit within this argumentation is a belief in the need to understand and evaluate the political dimensions of this broadening of semiotics, and navigate a way through its more complex politics. We said earlier that representational theory had filled the space of academic enquiry with an exhaustive account of the way that discourses are formulated and the cultural work they do. In terms of research, this has led to an eager search for the discursive content of heritage, wherever it might be found. This has been a largely successful line of enquiry, energized by Smith's (2006) formulation of the Authorized Heritage Discourse and subsequent applications of it in specific places as case studies (Ashton, 2009; Pendlebury, 2012; Waterton, 2010b; Ween, 2012). Where this kind of analysis would go next, however, is largely unclear, except to identify the variety of nuanced forms that it takes (see for example Watson, 2013). The application of more-than-representational theories in heritage, first through notions of performativity and later through affect and emotion, has at least provided a way forward. We should not, however, imagine that even this theoretical advance (see Chapter 2) has reached any particular milestone in its development – and that, for us, is really the point at this stage, and very much part of what this book has sought to explore.

So, with this challenge in mind, it is perhaps time to ask where these theoretical advances are taking us? Certainly in the first instance we should problematize the semiotic landscapes of heritage attractions and explore their new complexities. In this, the search for those discursive elements mentioned above should be combined with a notion of what else is constitutive and active in such landscapes, particularly in terms of what it or they are doing. This means looking at the subjective and intersubjective, and examining the ways in which emotions are provoked and affect manipulated, not as separate fields but rather as those in which representations are strongly implicated. We should therefore be prepared to search beyond the discursive for meaning, and indeed for a semiotic that is embodied and experiential. Finally, we should not assume that a broader semiotic involves a new politics or an apolitical stance. Indeed, the political economy of heritage tourism may not be unsettled by any of this new thinking, but it may allow a glimmer of hope for something more inclusive. This merits further examination, only a hint of which can be offered here, because it seems unlikely that an understanding of emotion and affect will automatically lead us to a more inclusive theorization of what heritage is and does. There is simply no basis for such a belief. Indeed, it is far more likely that the same dynamics that operate behind the scenes of representation and discourse will operate behind the scenes of engagement and performativity, limiting what is enactable, prescribing what is appropriate, writing or affording particular emotions and affects into its scripts. This brings us back to the ways in which discourse is implicated in the manipulation of affect and emotion: we might be more interested now in the spine-tingling moment of hearing the anthem and saluting the flag, but we remain mindful that the music is the same and so is the flag.

The real question is what a concern with the subjective and intersubjective, the embodied and the affective, allows into the semiotic landscape that we did not envision before. And for that, in truth, we do not as yet have an answer. Nor do we know how such additional aspects of experience are positioned in relation to the ideological discourses of heritage. Do they simply enhance them? Add another dimension? Or, indeed, strengthen them with another buttress against the possibility of oppositional values suddenly finding voice in the experience of heritage tourism? We have argued throughout this book that authorized heritage discourses both create and deplete meaning by projecting some things and ignoring (and therefore suppressing) others. But does the addition of an affective dimension to the semiotic landscape disrupt this or simply amplify it? We can easily accept that dominant discourses have power over text and textual meaning, but can these same discourses *affect* or is the latter in its embodied domain immune from the effects of discourse, the body's capacities beyond the semiotic call to action? Again, we do not yet have clear answers to this, but we have suggested that there is at least a raggedy line between the representational and more-than-representational, or perhaps more accurately, one that is quite porous, such that representation and performativity are much more closely connected and interconnected than the theoretical debate has tended to suggest thus far. We are reluctant to 'force the issue', however: far better to let a new research agenda do the talking.

Some Final Words . . .

New ideas, new fields and new contexts suggest, simultaneously, that there may be a need for new methods and much has already been said about what are arguably the limits of conventional research methods for exploring the affective domain. We do not pretend to resolve this conundrum here, but we do feel compelled to at least make a call to action in terms of addressing the pressing need for more research. What we are suggesting is that researchers interested in heritage tourism and its cognate fields should consider, as we have done, taking stock of the theoretical advances discussed in this book and explore the implications these have for their own research and associated methodological approaches. On this issue of method we are agnostic about the need for completely new ways of capturing and recording experiences at heritage sites. Rather, we feel that it is more realistic to push a little at what we already do under the umbrella of ethnography. Since we have never advocated positivistic research based on large-scale surveys or questionnaire-type research instruments, we are left with wondering what we might do differently on the qualitative side.

Our own thinking, as we have suggested here, has led us to explore the value of photography as an embodied act that links the representational with the performative and affective. Photographs, in many ways, provide a rich source of data that allow us to explore the manner in which people engage with heritage sites and how they enact their own responses to those sites. This turn to photography allows us to engage with, and continue to develop, our belief that research should capture moments of engagement and meaning *in situ*, and should empower respondents to identify for themselves what is significant about their engagements with objects, places and events. In this, we are firmly on board with David Crouch's (2011) assertion that it is what we do as a tourist, or what anybody does, how we feel and what meaning we derive, that matters. And for this, words alone may never be enough.

In this volume then, we have recognized and foregrounded the value of photographs as well as the practices of photograph*ing*, but we are mindful also that we should enable people to invest their experiences with feeling and intensity in other ways too, and, moreover, be prepared to capture or record this through observation, conversation and by sharing experiences with respondents, not as sneaky participant observers, but as collaborators, advocates, enablers, fellow travellers and tourists. In other words, our position is firmly that we should not separate ourselves from the experience of others but be a part of it in some way. Auto-ethnography, autophotography, performative ethnography, the 'go-along', 'walking with the people', video journals, researcher journals and so forth, therefore, have a strong place within the research scape we are imagining, as do immersive and expressive styles of writing that are openly subjective. But as we have argued throughout the volume that representational theory is being *added* to, rather than replaced, we also seek to align these new or nuanced methodological approaches with the tried and tested modalities of critical deconstruction and discourse analysis in order to engender an expanded semiotics. In common among these approaches, at their essence, is an engagement with practice-based methods that seek to capture, in the means that are available to us as social researchers, the here-and-now of experience. At its strongest, our point is that we should stop pretending that meaning can only be generated from 'research instruments' – unless of course we are taking up Longhurst *et al.*'s (2008: 215) call to use our bodies as 'instruments of research' – and instead recognize that the use of such things obscures as much as it reveals. We are not yet clear how the results of this kind of research should be presented, except that the methods of analysis should be transparent, bold and challenging in their deconstruction of assumptions, common sense and surface logic. The finer, practical workings of this imagination are perhaps for another volume.

We are mindful that we are drawing this volume to a close with a series of questions, but not, we hope, with the lingering taste of something written in the spirit of opposition. To the contrary, we have sought here to highlight much that is useful in the theories of representation, adding to them what we see as avenues of enquiry opened up by the more-than-representational that are well worth exploring. This may be the case for heritage tourism more than anywhere, as ours is a field that has rarely developed its theories in ways that could be construed as anything other than piecemeal, beginning with its initial operational perspectives to which frames of reference, drawn from sociology, anthropology and, latterly, cultural geography, have been added. For most of its (quite short) history, heritage 'theory' has provided little sense of direction and demonstrated even less momentum, though there have been milestone moments, of course, to which we have made reference. Theories in heritage studies, such as those concerned with commodification, authenticity and dissonance, have provided much of value, for example. Likewise, the post-structuralist modes of thinking associated with representational theory and discourse have brought a powerful, and enduring, basis for understanding the semiosis of heritage tourism in social, cultural and political contexts. Now we can take another step and explore a valuable seam of inquiry that places people and their moments of engagement at the centre of our studies. The embodied semiotics of such an experience have the potential to reveal layers of meaning that might otherwise never be examined, leaving the semiotic landscapes of heritage tourism even richer places than once they were.

References

Abu-Khafajah, S. (2010) Meaning-making and cultural heritage in Jordan: The local community, the contexts and the archaeological sites in Khreibt al-Suq. *International Journal of Heritage Studies* 16 (1), 123–139.
Adey, P. (2008) Airports, mobility and the calculative architecture of affective control. *Geoforum* 39 (1), 438–451.
Ahmed, S. (2004a) Affective economies. *Social Text* 22 (2), 117–139.
Ahmed, S. (2004b) Collective feelings or, the impressions left by others. *Theory, Culture and Society* 21 (2), 25–42.
Ahmed, S. and Stacey, J. (2001) Introduction: Dermographies. In S. Ahmed and J. Stacey (eds) *Thinking through the Skin* (pp. 1–17). London: Routledge.
Aitchison, C. (1999) New cultural geographies: The spatiality of leisure, gender and sexuality. *Leisure Studies* 18 (1), 19–39.
Aitchison, C. (2000) Poststructural feminist theories of representing Others: A response to the 'crisis' in leisure studies' discourse. *Leisure Studies* 19 (3), 127–144.
Albers, P.C. and James, W.R. (1988) Travel photography: A methodological approach. *Annals of Tourism Research* 15 (1), 134–158.
Allen, M.J. and Brown, S.D. (2011) Embodiment and living memorials: The affective labour of remembering the 2005 London bombings. *Memory Studies* 4 (3), 312–327.
Almeida Santos, C. (2004) Framing Portugal: Representational dynamics. *Annals of Tourism Research* 31 (1), 122–138.
Amoamo, M. and Thompson, A. (2010) (Re)Imaging Māori tourism: Representation and cultural hybridity in postcolonial New Zealand. *Tourist Studies* 10 (1), 35–55.
Anderson, B. (2004) Recorded music and practices of remembering. *Social and Cultural Geography* 5 (1), 3–20.
Anderson, B. (2006) Becoming and being hopeful: towards a theory of affect. *Environment and Planning D: Society and Space* 24 (5), 733–752.
Anderson, B. and Harrison, P. (2010) Questioning affect and emotion. *Area* 38 (3), 333–335.
Andrews, H. (2005) Feeling at home: Embodying Britishness in a Spanish charter tourist resort. *Tourist Studies* 5 (3), 247–266.
Arnould, E. and Price, L. (1993) River magic: Extraordinary experience and the extended service encounter. *Journal of Consumer Research* 20 (June), 24–45.
Ashton, P. (2009) The birthplace of Australian multiculturalism? Retrospective commemoration, participatory memorialisation and official heritage. *International Journal of Heritage Studies* 15 (5), 381–398.

Ashworth, G.J. and Tunbridge, J.E. (1990) *The Tourist Historic City, Retrospect and Prospect of Managing the Historic City*. London: Pergamon.
Bærenholdt, J., Haldrup, M., Larsen, J. and Urry, J. (2004) *Performing Tourist Places*. Aldershot and Burlington: Ashgate.
Bagnall, G. (2003) Performances and performativity at heritage sites. *Museums and Society* 1 (2), 87–103.
Bakhtin, M.M. (1981) (ed. M. Holquist, trans. C. Emerson) *The Dialogic Imagination: Four Essays*. Austin: University of Texas Press.
Barnett, C. (2008) Political affects in public spaces: normative blind-spots in non-representational ontologies. *Transactions of the Institute of British Geography* 33 (2), 186–200.
Baron, S., Harris, K. and Harris, R. (2001) Retail theatre: The intended effect of the performance. *Journal of Service Research* 4 (2), 102–117.
Barthes, R. (1985 [1964]) (trans. R. Howard) *The Rhetoric of the Image*. Berkeley: University of California Press.
Barthes, R. (1967) *Elements of Semiology*. NewYork: Hill and Wang.
Barthes, R. (1972) *Mythologies*. New York: Hill and Wang.
Bauman, Z. (2001) Consuming life. *Journal of Consumer Culture* 1 (1), 9–29.
Bauman, Z. (2007) *Consuming Life*. London: Polity Press.
Bell, C. and Lyall, J. (2002) The accelerated sublime, thrill-seeking adventure heroes in the commodified landscape. In S. Coleman and M. Crang (eds) *Tourism, Between Place and Performance* (pp. 21–37). Oxford: Berghahn Books.
Blommaert, J. (2005) *Discourse: A Critical Introduction*. Cambridge: Cambridge University Press.
Boorstin, D.J. (1961) *The Image: A Guide to Pseudo-Events in America*. New York: Harper and Row.
Brennan, T. (2004) *The Transmission of Affect*. Ithaca, NY: Cornell University Press.
Brett, D. (1996) *The Construction of Heritage*. Cork: Cork University Press.
Bruner, E.M. (2005) *Culture on Tour*. Chicago: University of Chicago.
Butler, J. (1990) *Gender Trouble: Feminism and the Subversion of Identity*. London: Routledge.
Butler, J. (1993) *Bodies that Matter: On the Discursive Limits of 'Sex'*. London: Routledge.
Butler, J. (1997) *Excitable Speech: A Politics of the Performative*. London: Routledge.
Butler, R.W. (1980) The concept of the tourist area life-cycle of evolution: Implications for management of resources. *Canadian Geographer* 24 (1), 5–12.
Cantwell, R. (1993) *Ethnomimesis*. Chapel Hill: University of North Carolina Press.
Carolan, M.S. (2008) More-than-representational knowledge/s of the countryside: How we think as bodies. *Sociologia Ruralis* 48 (4), 408–422.
Castree, N. and MacMillan, T. (2004) Old news: Representation and academic novelty. *Environment and Planning A* 36 (3), 469–480.
Chalfen, R. (1979) Photography's role in tourism: Some unexplored relationships. *Annals of Tourism Research* 6 (4), 435–447.
Chandler, J. (1993) *John Leland's Itinerary, Travels in Tudor England*. London: Sutton Publishing.
Clark, G. (1965) *Archaeology in Society*. London: Methuen and Co Ltd.
Cohen, E. (1988) Authenticity and commoditisation in tourism. *Annals of Tourism Research* 15 (3), 371–386.
Coleman, S. and Crang, M. (2002) Grounded tourists, travelling theory. In S. Coleman and M. Crang (eds) *Tourism: Between Place and Performance* (pp. 1–17). Oxford: Berghahn Books.
Connerton, P. (1989) *How Societies Remember*. Cambridge: Cambridge University Press.
Connerton, P. (2011) *The Spirit of Mourning: History, Memory and the Body*. Cambridge: Cambridge University Press.

Cook, G. (2001) *The Discourse of Marketing*. Abingdon: Routledge.
Copeland, T. (2010) Site seeing: Street walking through a low-visibility landscape. In E. Waterton and S. Watson (eds) *Culture, Heritage and Representation, Perspectives on Visuality and the Past* (pp. 229–247). Farnham: Ashgate.
Cox, C. (2011) Beyond representation and signification: Towards a sonic materialism. *Journal of Visual Culture* 10 (2), 145–161.
Crang, M. (1994) On the heritage trail: Maps of and journeys to Olde Englande. *Environment and Planning D: Society and Space* 12 (3), 341–355.
Crang, M. (1997) Picturing practices: Research through the tourist gaze. *Progress in Human Geography* 21 (3), 359–373.
Crouch, D. (2000) Places around us: Embodied lay geographies in leisure and tourism. *Leisure Studies* 19, 63–76.
Crouch, D. (2002) Surrounded by place: Embodied encounters. In S. Coleman and M. Crang (eds) *Tourism: Between Place and Performance* (pp. 207–218). New York: Berghahn Books.
Crouch, D. (2010a) The perpetual performance and emergence of heritage. In E. Waterton and S. Watson (eds) *Culture, Heritage and Representation, Perspectives on Visuality and the Past* (pp. 57–71). Farnham: Ashgate.
Crouch, D. (2010b) *Flirting with Space: Journeys and Creativity*. Aldershot: Ashgate.
Crouch, D. (2011) Book review: The tourist gaze 3.0. *Tourist Studies* 11 (3), 291–295.
Crouch, D. (2012) Meaning, encounter and performativity. In L. Smith, E. Waterton and S. Watson (eds) *The Cultural Moment in Tourism* (pp. 19–37). London: Routledge.
Crouch, D. and Lübbren, N. (2003) Introduction. In D. Crouch and N. Lübbren (eds) *Visual Culture and Tourism* (pp. 1–20). Oxford: Berg.
Crouch, D. Aronsson, L. and Wahlström, L. (2001) Tourist encounters. *Tourist Studies* 1 (3), 253–270.
Culler, J. (1976) *Saussure*. London: Fontana.
Culler, J. (1990) The semiotics of tourism. In *Framing the Sign: Criticism and Its Institutions*. Boulder: University of Colorado Press.
Curti, G.H. (2008) From a wall of bodies to a body of walls: Politics of affect/politics of memory/politics of war. *Emotion, Space and Society* 1 (2), 106–118.
Dann, G.M.S. (1986) *The Language of Tourism*. Wallingford: CABI.
Dann, G.M.S. (1996) The people of tourist brochures. In T. Selwyn (ed.) *The Tourist Image: Myths and Myth Making in Tourism* (pp. 61–81). London: Wiley.
de Saussure, F. (1915 [1966]) (trans. Wade Baskin) *Cour de Linguistique Generate (Course in General Linguistics)*. New York: McGraw-Hill.
Degen, M.M. and Rose, G. (2012) The sensory experiencing of urban design: The role of walking and perceptual memory. *Urban Studies* 49 (15), 3271–3287.
Delafons, J. (1997) *Politics and Preservation: A Policy History of the Built Heritage, 1882–1996*. London: Chapman and Hall.
Deleuze, G. and Guattari, F. (2004) *A Thousand Plateaus*. London: Continuum.
Dicks, B. (2000) *Heritage, Place and Community*. Cardiff: University of Wales Press.
Dixon, D. and Jones, J.P. (2004) Poststructuralism. In J. Duncan, N. Duncan and R. Schein (eds) *A Companion to Cultural Geography* (pp. 79–107). Minneapolis: University of Minnesota Press.
Echtner, C.M. (1999) The semiotic paradigm: Implications for tourism research. *Tourism Management* 20 (1), 47–57.
Edensor, T. (1997) National identity and the politics of memory: Remembering Bruce and Wallace in symbolic space. *Environment and Planning D: Society and Space* 15 (2), 175–194.

Edensor, T. (2001) Performing tourism, staging tourism: (Re)producing tourist space and practice. *Tourist Studies* 1 (1), 59–81.
Edensor, T. (2002) *National Identity, Popular Culture and Everyday Life*. Oxford: Berg.
Edensor, T. (2005) *Industrial Ruins: Space, Aesthetics and Materiality*. Oxford: Berg.
Edensor, T. (ed.) (2010a) *Geographies of Rhythm*. Aldershot: Ashgate.
Edensor, T. (2010b) Introduction: Thinking about rhythm and space. In T. Edensor (ed.) *Geographies of Rhythm* (pp. 1–19). Aldershot: Ashgate.
Edwards, E. (1996) Postcards: Greetings from another world. In T. Selwyn (ed.) *The Tourist Image: Myths and Myth Making in Tourism* (pp. 197–222). London: Wiley.
Edwards, E. (2012) Objects of affect: Photography beyond the image. *Annual Review of Anthropology* 41, 221–234.
Enloe, C. (1989) *Bananas, Beaches and Bases: Making Feminist Sense of International Politics*. Pandora: London.
Fairclough, N. (2008) A dialectical-relational approach to critical discourse analysis in social research. In R. Wodak and M. Meyer (eds) *Methods of Critical Discourse Analysis* (pp. 162–186). London: SAGE.
Fairclough, N., Graham, P., Lemke, J. and Wodak, R. (2004) Introduction. *Critical Discourse Studies* 1 (1), 1–7.
Feighery, W. (2009) Tourism, stock photography and surveillance: A Foucauldian interpretation. *Journal of Tourism and Cultural Change* 7 (3), 161–178.
Foote, K.E. and Azaryahu, M. (2009) Semiotics. In R. Kitchin and N. Thrift (eds) *International Encyclopaedia of Human Geography* (pp. 89–95). Oxford: Elsevier.
Foucault, M. (1970) *The Order of Things: An Archaeology of the Human Sciences*. London: Tavistock.
Foucault, M. (1977) Nietzsche, genealogy and history. In D. Bouchard (ed.) *Language, Counter-Memory, Practice: Selected Essays and Interviews* (pp. 139–164). New York: Cornell University Press.
Foucault, M. (1980) Truth and power. In C. Gordon (ed.) *Power/Knowledge: Selected Interviews and Other Writings 1972–1977* (pp. 109–133). Brighton: Harvester.
Foucault, M. (1984) The order of discourse. In M. Shapiro (ed.) *Language and Politics* (pp. 108–138). Oxford: Basil Blackwell.
Foucault, M. (2003) *The Archaeology of Knowledge*. London: Routledge Classics.
Franklin, A. (2003) *Tourism, An Introduction*. London: SAGE.
French, B.M. (2012) The semiotics of collective memory. *Annual Review of Anthropology* 41, 337–353.
Freeman, C.G. (2010) Photosharing on Flickr: Intangible heritage and emergent publics. *International Journal of Heritage Studies* 16 (4–5), 352–368.
Game, A. (1991) *Undoing the Social: Towards a Deconstructive Sociology*. Milton Keynes: Open University Press.
Garrod, B. (2009) Understanding the relationship between tourism destination imagery and tourist photography. *Journal of Travel Research* 47 (3), 346–358.
Giblin, J. (2013) Post-conflict heritage: Symbolic healing and cultural renewal. *International Journal of Heritage Studies*. iFirst: DOI:10.1080/13527258.2013.772912.
Gilpin, W. (1769 [1802]) *An Essay on Prints* (5th edn). London: Cadell and Davies.
Gilpin, W. (1792 [1808]) *Three Essays on Picturesque Beauty on Picturesque Travel and on Sketching Landscape, with a Poem on Landscape Painting*. London: Cadell and Davies.
Girman, C. (2012) Diaries, dicks, and desire: How the leaky traveler troubles dominant discourse in the eroticized Caribbean. *Journal of Tourism and Cultural Change* 10 (1), 34–50.

Gorton, K. (2007) Theorizing emotion and affect: Feminist engagements. *Feminist Theory* 8, 333–348.
Graburn, N. (1989) Tourism: The sacred journey. In V. Smith (ed.) *Hosts and Guests: The Anthropology of Tourism* (pp. 21–36). Philadelphia: University of Pennsylvania Press.
Gregg, M. and Seigworth, G.J. (eds) (2010) *The Affect Theory Reader*. Durham, NC: Duke University Press.
Grydehøj, A. (2010) Uninherited heritage: Tradition and heritage production in Shetland, Åland and Svalbard. *International Journal of Heritage Studies* 16 (1–2), 77–89.
Hajer, M. (1995) *The Politics of Environmental Discourse: Ecological Modernization and the Policy Process*. Oxford: Claredon Press.
Haldrup, M. (2009) Banal tourism? Between cosmopolitanism and Orientalism. In P.O. Pons, M. Crang and P. Travlou (eds) *Cultures of Mass Tourism: Doing the Mediterranean in the Age of Banal Mobilities* (pp. 53–74). Farnham: Ashgate.
Haldrup, M. and Bærenholdt, J.O. (in press) Heritage as performance. In E. Waterton and S. Watson (eds) *The Palgrave Handbook of Contemporary Heritage Research*. Basingstoke: Palgrave Macmillan.
Haldrup, M. and Larsen, J. (2003) The family gaze. *Tourist Studies* 3 (1), 23–46.
Haldrup, M. and Larsen, J. (2006) Material cultures of tourism. *Leisure Studies* 25 (3), 275–289.
Hall, S. (1997) *Representation: Cultural Representations and Signifying Practices*. London: SAGE.
Harrison, R. (2012) Forgetting to remember, remembering to forget: Late modern heritage practices, sustainability and the 'crisis' of accumulation of the past. *International Journal of Heritage Studies*. iFirst: DOI: 10.1080/13527258.2012.678371.
Harvey, D.C. (2001) Heritage pasts and heritage presents: Temporality, meaning and the scope for heritage studies. *International Journal of Heritage Studies* 7 (4), 319–338.
Hayes-Conroy, J. and Hayes-Conroy, A. (2010) Visceral geographies: Mattering, relating and defying. *Geography Compass* 4 (9), 1273–1283.
Healy, C. (2008) *Forgetting Aborigines*. Sydney: UNSW Press.
Herbert, D.T. (1995) *Heritage, Tourism and Society*. London: Mansell.
Herbert, D.T., Prentice, R.C. and Thomas, C.J. (eds) (1989) *Heritage Sites: Strategies for Marketing and Development*. Aldershot: Ashgate.
Heritage Lottery Fund (2010) *Investing in Success, Heritage and the UK Tourism Economy*. HLF/Visit Britain.
Hobsbawm, E. and Ranger, T. (eds) (1983) *The Invention of Tradition*. Oxford: Blackwell.
Hoelscher, S. and Alderman, D.H. (2004) Memory and place: Geographies of a critical relationship. *Social and Cultural Geography* 5 (3), 347–355.
Hopley, C. and Mahony, P. (2011) Marketing sense of place in the forest of Bowland. In J. Schofield and R. Szymanski (eds) *Local Heritage, Global Context, Cultural Perspectives on Sense of Place* (pp. 33–51). Farnham: Ashgate.
Hsiu-yen Yeh, J. (2009) The embodiment of sociability through the tourist camera. In M. Robinson and D. Picard (eds) *The Framed World: Tourism, Tourists and Photography* (pp. 199–216). Farnham: Ashgate.
Hughes, G. (1998) Tourism and the realization of space. In G. Ringer (ed.) *Destinations: Cultural Landscapes of Tourism* (pp. 17–32). London: Routledge.
Ingold, T. (1995) Building, dwelling, living: How animals and people make themselves at home. In M. Strathern (ed.) *Shifting Contexts: Transformations in Anthropological Knowledge* (pp. 57–80). London: Routledge.

Irving, W. (1832) *Tales of the Alhambra*. New York: Lea and Carey.
Irwin, R. (2004) *The Alhambra*. London: Profile Books.
Jack, G. and Phipps, A. (2005) *Tourism and Intercultural Exchange: Why Tourism Matters*. Clevedon: Channel View Publications.
Jacobs, J.M. and Nash, C. (2003) Too little, too much: Cultural feminist geographies. *Gender, Place and Culture* 10 (3), 265–279.
Jaworski, A. and Pritchard, A. (2005) *Discourse, Communication and Tourism*. Clevedon: Channel View Publications.
Jay, M. (1988) Scopic regimes of modernity. In H. Foster (ed.) *Vision and Visuality: Discussions in Contemporary Culture* (pp. 3–23). New York: The New Press.
Jay, M. (1996) Vision in context: Reflections and refractions. In T. Brennan and M. Jay (eds) *Vision in Context: Historical and Contemporary Perspectives on Sight* (pp. 1–12). London: Routledge.
Jenkins, O.H. (2003) Photography and travel brochures: The circle of representation. *Tourism Geographies* 5 (3), 305–328.
Jolliffe, L. (2007) *Tea and Tourism: Tourists, Traditions and Transformations*. Clevedon: Channel View Publications.
Jolliffe, L. (2010) *Coffee Culture, Destinations and Tourism*. Bristol: Channel View Publications.
Jolliffe, L. (2012) *Sugar Heritage and Tourism in Transition*. Bristol: Channel View Publications.
Jones, O. (2003) 'Endlessly revisited and forever gone': On memory, reverie and emotional imagination in doing children's geographies. An 'Addendum' to '"To go back up the side hill": Memories, imaginations and reveries of childhood' by C. Philo. *Children's Geographies* 1 (1), 25–36.
Jones, O. (2005) An ecology of emotion, memory, self and landscape. In J. Davidson, L. Bondi and M. Smith (eds) *Emotional Geographies* (pp. 205–218). Aldershot: Ashgate.
Jones, O. (2011) Geography, memory and non-representational geographies. *Geography Compass* 5 (12), 875–885.
Jones, R. (2010) Authenticity, the media and heritage tourism: Robin Hood and Brother Caedfel as midlands tourist magnets. In E. Waterton and S. Watson (eds) *Culture, Heritage and Representation: Perspectives on Visuality and the Past* (pp. 145–154). Farnham: Ashgate.
Keane, W. (2003) Semiotics and the social analysis of material things. *Language and Communication* 23 (3), 409–425.
Kirshenblatt-Gimblett, B. (1998) *Destination Culture, Tourism, Museums and Heritage*. Berkeley: University of California Press.
Knudsen, B.T. and Waade, A.M. (2010) *Re-Investing Authenticity: Tourism, Place and Emotions*. Bristol: Channel View Publications.
Kopytoff, I. (1986) The cultural biography of things: Commoditisation as process. In A. Appadurai (ed.) *The Social Life of Things: Commodities in Cultural Perspective* (pp. 64–91). Cambridge: Cambridge University Press.
Kress, G. and van Leeuwen, T. (2006) *Reading Images: The Grammar of Visual Design*. London: Routledge.
Krishna, A. (ed.) (2010) *Sensory Marketing: Research on the Sensuality of Products*. London: Routledge.
Kristeva, J. (1980) *Desire in Language: A Semiotic Approach to Literature and Art*. New York: Columbia University.
Lane, R. and Waitt, G. (2001) Authenticity in tourism and Native Title: Place, time and spatial politics in the East Kimberleys. *Social and Cultural Geography* 2 (4), 381–405.
Larsen, J. (2005) Families seen sightseeing. *Space and Culture* 8 (4), 416–434.

Larsen, J. (2006) Geographies of tourism photography: Choreographies and performances. In J. Falkheimer and A. Jansson (eds) *Geographies of Communication: The Spatial Turn in Media Studies* (pp. 243–261). Gøteborg: NORDICOM.
Larsen, J. (2008a) Practices and flows of digital photography: An ethnographic framework. *Mobilities* 3 (1), 141–160.
Larsen, J. (2008b) De-exoticizing tourist travel: Everyday life and sociality on the move. *Leisure Studies* 27 (1), 21–34.
Larsen, J. and Urry, J. (2011) Gazing and performing. *Environment and Planning D: Society and Space* 29 (6), 1110–1125.
Lash, S. and Urry, J. (1994) *Economies of Signs and Space*. London: SAGE.
Latham, A. and McCormack, D.P. (2009) Thinking with images in non-representational cities: Vignettes from Berlin. *Area* 41 (3), 252–262.
Lawrence, R. and Gibson, C. (2007) Obliging Indigenous citizens? *Cultural Studies* 21 (4–5), 650–671.
Lazar, M.M. (2000) Gender, discourse and semiotics: The politics of parenthood representations. *Discourse and Society* 11 (3), 373–400.
Lefebvre, H. (1991) *The Production of Space*. London: Wiley.
Lefebvre, H. (2004) *Rythmanalysis: Space, Time and Everyday Life*. London: Continuum.
Lévi-Strauss, C. (1963) *Structural Anthropology*. New York: Basic Books.
Levy, S.J. (1959) Symbols for sale. *Harvard Business Review* 37 (July), 117–124.
Light, D. (2012) Taking Dracula on holiday: The presence of 'home' in the tourist encounter. In L. Smith, E. Waterton and S. Watson (eds) *The Cultural Moment in Tourism* (pp. 59–78). London: Routledge.
Light, D. and Prentice, R.C. (1994) Who consumes the heritage product? Implications for European heritage tourism. In G.J. Ashworth and P.J. Larkham (eds) *Building a New Heritage, Tourism, Culture and Identity in the New Europe* (pp. 90–116). London: Routledge.
Little, K. (2010) Paradise from the other side of nowhere: Troubling a troubled scene of tourist encounter in Belize. *Journal of Tourism and Cultural Change* 8 (1–2), 1–14.
Longhurst, R., Ho, E. and Johnston, L. (2008) Using 'the body' as an 'instrument of research': kimch'I and pavlova. *Area* 40 (2), 208–217.
Lorimer, H. (2005) Cultural geography: The busyness of being 'more than representational'. *Progress in Human Geography* 29 (1), 83–94.
MacCannell, D. (1973) Staged authenticity: Arrangements of social space in social settings. *American Journal of Sociology* 79 (3), 589–603.
MacCannell, D. (1976) *The Tourist: A New Theory of the Leisure Class*. Berkeley and Los Angeles: University of California Press.
MacCannell, D. (1989) Introduction. *Annals of Tourism Research* 16, 1–6.
MacCannell, D. (2011) *The Ethics of Sightseeing*. Los Angeles: University of California Press.
MacDonald, F. (2002) The Scottish Highlands as spectacle. In S. Coleman and M. Crang (eds) *Tourism, Between Place and Performance* (pp. 54–72). Oxford: Berghahn Books.
Macdonald, S. (2013) *Memorylands: Heritage and Identity in Europe Today*. London: Routledge.
Marston, G. (2004) *Social Policy and Discourse Analysis: Policy Change in Public Housing*. Hants: Ashgate Publishing Limited.
Marwick, K. (2001) Postcards from Malta: Image, consumption, context. *Annals of Tourism Research* 28 (2), 417–438.
Massey, D. (2005) *For Space*. London: SAGE.

Mellinger, W. (1994) Toward a critical analysis of tourism representations. *Annals of Tourism Research* 21 (4), 756–779.
Metro-Roland, M. (2009) Interpreting meaning: An application of Peircean semiotics to tourism. *Tourism Geographies* 11 (2), 270–279.
Metusela, C. and Waitt, G. (2012) *Tourism and Australian Beach Cultures: Revealing Bodies.* Bristol: Channel View Publications.
Metz, C. (1977) (trans. C. Britton, A. Williams, B. Brewster and A. Guzzetti) *The Imaginary Signifier: Psychoanalysis and the Cinema.* Bloomington and Indianapolis: Indiana University Press.
Mick, D.G. (1986) Consumer research and semiotics: Exploring the morphology of signs, symbols and significance. *Journal of Consumer Research* 13 (2), 196–213.
Mick, D.G. and McQuarrie, E.F. (1996) Figures of rhetoric in advertising language. *Journal of Consumer Research* 22 (4), 424–438.
Mick, D.G., Burroughs, J.E., Hetzel, P. and Brannen, M.Y. (2004) Pursuing the meaning of meaning in the commercial world: An international review of marketing and consumer research founded on semiotics. *Semiotica* 24, June. [Online]. See http://ssrn.com/abstract = 550508 (accessed 9 January 2013).
Moi, T. (1986) (ed.) *The Kristeva Reader.* London: Wiley-Blackwell.
Moore, N. and Whelan, Y. (2007) *Heritage, Memory and the Politics of Identity: New Perspectives on the Cultural Landscape.* Aldershot: Ashgate.
Mordue, T. (2005) Tourism, performance and social exclusion in 'Olde Yorke'. *Annals of Tourism Research* 32 (1), 179–198.
Mordue, T. (2010) Time machines and spacecraft: Navigating the spaces of heritage tourism performance. In E. Waterton and S. Watson (eds) *Culture, Heritage and Representation, Perspectives on Visuality and the Past* (pp. 173–194). Farnham: Ashgate.
Morgan, N. and Pritchard, A. (1998) *Tourism Promotion and Power: Creating Images, Creating Identities.* Chichester: Wiley.
Neumann, M. (2002) Making the scene, the poetics and performances of displacement at the Grand Canyon. In S. Coleman and M. Crang (eds) *Tourism, Between Place and Performance* (pp. 38–53). Oxford: Berghahn Books.
Nora, P. (1989) Between memory and history: *Les Lieux de Mémoire* (trans. M. Roudebush), 26 (Spring), 7–25.
Obrador Pons, P. (2003) Being-on-holiday: Tourist dwelling, bodies and place. *Tourist Studies* 3 (1), 47–66.
O'Dowd, M. (2009) Place, identity and nationhood: The northern territory intervention as the final act of a dying nation. *Continuum: Journal of Media & Cultural Studies* 23 (6), 803–825.
Ogilvie, M. and Mizerski, K. (2011) Using semiotics in consumer research to understand everyday phenomena. *International Journal of Market Research* 53 (5), 651–668.
Osborne, P.D. (2000) *Travelling Light: Photography, Travel and Visual Culture.* Manchester: Manchester University Press.
Oswald, A. Ainsworth, S. and Pearson, T. (2007) *Hillforts, Prehistoric Strongholds of Northumberland National Park.* London: English Heritage.
Palmer, C. (2005) An ethnography of Englishness: Experiencing identity through tourism. *Annals of Tourism Research* 32 (1), 7–27.
Palmer, C. (2009) Moving with the times: Visual representations of the tourist phenomenon. *Journal of Tourism Consumption and Practice* 1 (1), 74–85.

Paschen, J-A. (2010) Decolonising the gaze at Uluru (Ayers Rock). In P. Burns, C. Palmer and J-A. Lester (eds) *Tourism and Visual Culture. Volume 1: Theories and Concepts*. Wallingford: CABI.

Pendlebury, J. (2012) Conservation values, the authorised heritage discourse and the conservation-planning assemblage. *International Journal of Heritage Studies*. iFirst: DOI: 10.1080/13527258.2012.700282.

Pennington, J.W. and Thomsen, R.C. (2010) A semiotic model of destination representations applied to cultural and heritage tourism marketing. *Scandinavian Journal of Hospitality and Tourism* 10 (1), 33–53.

Picard, D. and Robinson, M. (eds) (2012) *Emotion in Motion: Tourism, Affect and Transformation*. Aldershot: Ashgate.

Piggott, S. (1989) *Ancient Britons and the Antiquarian Imagination, Ideas from the Renaissance to the Regency*. London: Thames and Hudson.

Pike, S. (2002) Destination image analysis: A review of 142 papers from 1973 to 2000. *Tourism Management* 23 (5), 541–549.

Pile, S. (2010) Emotions and affect in recent human geography. *Transactions of the Institute of British Geographers* 35 (1), 5–20.

Pine, B.J. and Gilmore, J.H. (2011) *The Experience Economy*. Harvard Business Review Press.

Pons, P. (2003) Being-in-tourism: Tourist dwelling, bodies and places. *Tourist Studies* 3 (3), 47–66.

Porter, L. (2010) *Unlearning the Colonial Cultures of Planning*. Aldershot: Ashgate.

Potter, F.J. (2005) *The History of Gothic Publishing 1800–1835: Exhuming the Trade*. London: Palgrave Macmillan.

Prendergast, C. (2000) *The Triangle of Representation*. New York: Columbia University Press.

Pritchard, A. and Morgan, N. (2003) Mythic geographies of representation and identity: Contemporary postcards of Wales. *Journal of Tourism and Cultural Change* 1 (2), 111–130.

Pritchard, A. and Morgan, N. (2010) 'Wild On' the beach: Discourses of desire, sexuality and liminality. In E. Waterton and S. Watson (eds) *Culture, Heritage and Representation: Perspectives on Visuality and the Past* (pp. 127–143). Farnham: Ashgate.

Radford, G.P. and Radford, M.L. (2005) Structuralism, post-structuralism, and the library: de Saussure and Foucault. *Journal of Documentation* 61 (1), 60–78.

Read, P. (2000) *Belonging: Australians, Place and Aboriginal Ownership*. Cambridge: Cambridge University Press.

Relph, E. (1976) *Place and Placelessness*. London: Pion.

Reynaud, A.T.J. (2004) Migrants' accounts of Rio: The contribution of affect to remembering place. *Space and Culture* 7 (1), 9–19.

Reynolds, F. (2004) The Director General's Statement. *The National Trust Report and Accounts 2003/04*. http://www.nationaltrust.org.uk/main/2004_dg_statement.pdf (accessed 12 October 2006).

Riley, W. (1934) *The Yorkshire Pennine's of the North West*. London: Herbert Jenkins Ltd.

Roberts, E. (2012) Geography and the visual image: A hautological approach. *Progress in Human Geography* [Online]. iFirst: DOI: 10.1177/0309132512460902.

Robinson, M. (2012) The emotional tourism. In D. Picard and M. Robinson (eds) *Emotions in Motions: Tourism, Affect and Transformation* (pp. 21–47). Farnham: Ashgate.

Robinson, M. and Picard, D. (2009) Moments, magic and memories: Photographing tourists, tourist photographs and making worlds. In M. Robinson and D. Picard (eds) *The Framed World: Tourism, Tourists and Photography* (pp. 1–37). Aldershot: Ashgate.

Rojek, C. (1997) Indexing, dragging and a social construction of tourist sites. In C. Rojek and J. Urry (eds) *Touring Cultures: Transformations of Travel Theory* (pp. 52–74). London: Routledge.
Rose, M. (2002) Landscape and labyrinths. *Geoforum* 33 (4), 455–467.
Rossi, L-M. (2010) Daughters of privilege: Class, sexuality, affect and the *Gilmore Girls*. In M. Liljeström and S. Paasonen (eds) *Working with Affect in Feminist Readings* (pp. 85–98). London: Routledge.
Said, E. (1978) *Orientalism*. New York: Pantheon Books.
Said, E. (1995) *Orientalism: Western Conceptions of the Orient*. Harmondsworth: Penguin Books.
Samuel, R. (1999) *Island Stories, Unravelling Britain. Theatres of Memory* (Vol. 2). London: Verso Books.
Sather-Wagstaff, J. (2011) *Heritage that Hurts: Tourists in the Memoryscapes of September 11*. Walnut Creek: Left Coast Press.
Scarles, C. (2009) Becoming tourist: Renegotiating the visual in the tourist experience. *Environment and Planning D: Society and Space* 27 (3), 465–488.
Scarles, C. (2010) Where words fail, visuals ignite: Opportunities for visual autoethnography in tourism research. *Annals of Tourism Research* 37 (4), 905–926.
Schirato, T. and Webb, J. (2004) *Understanding Visual Culture*. London: SAGE.
Schirato, T. and Webb, J. (2010) Inside/outside: Ways of seeing the world. In E. Waterton and S. Watson (eds) *Culture, Heritage and Representation: Perspectives on Visuality and the Past* (pp. 20–37). Farnham: Ashgate.
Schnapp, A. (1996) *The Discovery of the Past*. London: British Museum Press.
Schofield, J. and Szymanski, R. (eds) (2011) *Local Heritage, Global Context, Cultural Perspectives on Sense of Place*. Farnham: Ashgate.
Schwyzer, P. (1999) The scouring of the White Horse: Archaeology, identity and 'heritage'. *Representations* 65, 42–62.
Scollon, R. and Scollon, S.W. (2003) *Discourses in Place, Language in the Material World*. London: Routledge.
Scott, A. (2012) Publics versus professionals: Agency and engagement with 'Robin Hood' and the 'Pilgrim Fathers' in Nottinghamshire. In L. Smith, E. Waterton and S. Watson (eds) *The Cultural Moment in Tourism* (pp. 131–158). London: Routledge.
Scott, H.V. (2009) Representations, the politics of. In R. Kitchin and N. Thrift (eds) *International Encyclopaedia of Human Geography*. Elsevier. [Online]. See http://www.kriso.ee/international-encyclopedia-human-geography-db-9780080449111.html (accessed 9 January 2013).
Seamon, D. and Sowers, J. (2008) Edward Relph, place and placelessness. In P. Hubbard, R. Kitchen and G. Valentine (eds) *Key Texts in Human Geography* (pp. 43–52). London: Sage.
Selby, M. (2003) *Understanding Urban Tourism: Image, Culture and Experience*. I.B. Tauris and Co.
Selby, M. (2004) Consuming cities: Conceptualising and researching urban tourist knowledge. *Tourism Geographies* 6 (2), 186–207.
Selby, M. (2010) People-place-ast: The visitor experience of cultural heritage. In E. Waterton and S. Watson (eds) *Culture, Heritage and Representation: Perspectives on Visuality and the Past* (pp. 39–55). Farnham: Ashgate.
Selwyn, T. (1996) (ed.) *The Tourist Image: Myths and Myth Making in Tourism*. Chichester: Wiley.
Selwyn, T. (2010) The tourist as juggler in the hall of mirrors: Looking through images at the self. In E. Waterton and S. Watson (eds) *Culture, Heritage and Representation: Perspectives on Visuality and the Past* (pp. 194–214). Farnham: Ashgate.

Shields, R. (1991) *Places on the Margin, Alternative Geographies of Modernity*. London: Routledge.
Shostack, G.L. (1977) Breaking free from product marketing. *Journal of Marketing* 42 (2), 73–80.
Sirgy, M.J. and Su, C. (2000) Destination image, self-congruity and travel behaviour: Toward an integrative model. *Journal of Travel Research* 38 (4), 340–352.
Smith, L. (2006) *Uses of Heritage*. London: Routledge.
Smith, L. and Waterton, E. (2009) *Heritage, Communities and Archaeology*. London: Duckworth Press.
Smith, L. Cubitt, G., Wilson, R. and Fouseki, K (eds) (2011) *Representing Enslavement and Abolition in Museums*. London: Routledge.
Stewart, K. (2007) *Ordinary Affects*. Durham, NC: Duke University Press.
Sturken, M. and Cartwright, L. (2009) *Practices of Looking: An Introduction to Visual Culture*. Oxford: Oxford University Press.
Sundén, J. (2010) A sense of play: Affect, emotion and embodiment in *World of Warcraft*. In M. Liljeström and S. Paasonen (eds) *Working with Affect in Feminist Readings* (pp. 45–57). London: Routledge.
Taylor, S. (2001) Locating and conducting discourse analytic research. In M. Wetherell, S. Taylor and S.J. Yates (eds) *Discourse as Data: A Guide for Analysis* (pp. 5–48). London: SAGE.
Thien, D. (2005) After or beyond feeling? A consideration of affect and emotion in geography. *Area* 37 (4), 450–456.
Thompson, C. (2007) *The Suffering Traveller and the Romantic Imagination*. Oxford: Oxford University Press.
Thrift, N.J. (2004) Intensities of feeling: towards a spatial politics of affect. *Geografiska Annaler* 86 (1), 57–78.
Thrift, N.J. (2008) *Non-Representational Theories*. London: Routledge.
Thrift, N.J. and Dewsbury, J-D. (2000) Dead geographies? And how to make them live. *Environment and Planning D: Society and Space* 18 (4), 411–432.
Tilley, C. (2006) Introduction, identity, place, landscape and heritage. *Journal of Material Culture* 11 (7), 7–32.
Tolia-Kelly, D. (2007) Fear in paradise: The affective registers of the English Lake District landscape re-visited. *Senses and Society* 2 (3), 329–351.
Tolia-Kelly, D. (2012) Landscape and memory. In P. Howard, I. Thompson and E. Waterton(eds) *The Routledge Companion to Landscape Studies* (pp. 322–334). London: Routledge.
Travlou, P. (2002) Go Athens: A journey to the centre of the city. In S. Coleman and M. Crang (eds) *Tourism, Between Place and Performance* (pp. 108–128). Oxford: Berghahn Books.
Tunbridge, J.E. and Ashworth, G.J. (1995) *Dissonant Heritage: The Management of the Past as a Resource in Conflict*. London: John Wiley and Sons.
Urry, J. (1990) *The Tourist Gaze: Leisure and Travel in Contemporary Societies*. London: SAGE.
Urry, J. (2002) *The Tourist Gaze*. London: SAGE.
Urry, J. and Larsen, J. (2011) *The Tourist Gaze 3.0*. London: SAGE.
van den Abbeele, G. (1980) Sightseers: The tourist as theorist. *Diacritics* 10, 2–14.
van Dijck, J. (2008) Digital photography: Communication, identity, memory. *Visual Communication* 7 (1), 57–76.
van Leeuwen, T. (2005) *Introducing Social Semiotics*. London: Routledge.
Veblen, T. (2007 [1899]) *The Theory of the Leisure Class*. New York: Cosimo Inc.
Veijola, S. and Jokinen, E. (1994) The body in tourism. *Theory, Culture and Society* 11 (3), 125–151.

Waade, A.M. and Jørgensen, U.A. (2010) Haptic routes and digestive destinations in cooking series: images of food and place in *Keith Floyd* and *The Hairy Bikers* in relation to art history. *Journal of Tourism and Cultural Change* 8 (1–2), 84–100.
Walsh, K. (1992) *The Representation of the Past: Museums and Heritage in the Postmodern World*. London: Routledge.
Waterton, E. (2009) Sights of sites: Picturing heritage, power and exclusion. *Journal of Heritage Tourism* 4 (1), 37–56.
Waterton, E. (2010a) Branding the past: The visual imagery of England's heritage. In E. Waterton and S. Watson (eds) *Culture, Heritage and Representation: Perspectives on Visuality and the Past* (pp. 155–172). Farnham: Ashgate.
Waterton, E. (2010b) *Policy, Politics and the Discourses of Heritage in Britain*. London: Palgrave Macmillan.
Waterton, E. (2011) The burden of knowing versus the privilege of unknowing. In L. Smith, G. Cubitt, R. Wilson and K. Fouseki (eds) *Representing Enslavement and Abolition in Museums: Ambiguous Engagements* (pp. 23–43). London: Routledge.
Waterton, E. (2013) Heritage tourism and its representations. In R. Staiff, R. Bushell and S. Watson (eds) *Heritage and Tourism: Place, Encounter, Engagement* (pp. 64–84). London: Routledge.
Waterton, E. and Watson, S. (eds) (2010) *Culture, Heritage and Representation: Perspectives on Visuality and the Past*. Farnham: Ashgate.
Waterton, E. and Watson, S. (2012) Shades of the Caliphate: The cultural moment in Southern Spain. In L. Smith, E. Waterton and S. Watson (eds) *The Cultural Moment in Tourism* (pp. 161–181). London: Routledge.
Waterton, E. and Watson, S. (2013) Framing theory: Towards a critical imagination in heritage studies. *International Journal of Heritage Studies* 19 (6), 546–561.
Waterton, E., Smith, L., Wilson, R. and Fouseki, K. (2010) Forgetting to heal: Remembering the Abolition Act of 1807. *European Journal of English Studies* 14 (1), 23–36.
Watson, S. (2009) Archaeology, visuality and the negotiation of heritage. In E. Waterton and L. Smith (eds) *Taking Archaeology Out Of Heritage* (pp. 29–47). Newcastle-upon-Tyne: Cambridge Scholars Publishing.
Watson, S. (2010) Constructing Rhodes: Heritage tourism and visuality. In E. Waterton and S. Watson (eds) *Culture, Heritage and Representation: Perspectives on Visuality and the Past* (pp. 249–270). Farnham: Ashgate.
Watson, S. (2013) Country matters: The rural-historic as an authorised heritage discourse in England. In R. Staiff, R. Bushel and S.Watson (eds) *Heritage and Tourism, Place, Encounter, Engagement* (pp. 103–126). London: Routledge.
Watson S. and Waterton, E. (2010a) Reading the visual: Representation and narrative in the construction of heritage. *Material Culture Review* 71 (Spring), 84–97.
Watson, S. and Waterton, E. (2010b) Introduction: A visual heritage. In E. Waterton and S. Watson (eds) *Culture, Heritage and Representation: Perspectives on Visuality and the Past* (pp. 1–16). Farnham: Ashgate.
Webb, J. (2009) *Understanding Representation*. London: SAGE.
Ween, G.B. (2012) World Heritage and Indigenous rights: Norwegian examples. *International Journal of Heritage Studies* 18 (3), 257–270.
Whatmore, S. (1999) Hybrid geographies: Rethinking the human in human geography. In D. Massey, J. Allen and P. Sarre (eds) *Human Geography Today* (pp. 22–40). Cambridge: Polity.
White, G. (2006) Epilogue: Memory moments. *Ethos* 34 (2), 325–341.
Williams, R. (1977) *Marxism and Literature*. Oxford: Oxford University Press.

Wilson, R. (2013) *Cultural Heritage of the Great War in Britain*. Aldershot: Ashgate.
Winter, T. (2004) Landscape, memory and heritage: New Year celebrations at Angkor, Cambodia. *Current Issues in Tourism* 7 (4–5): 330–345.
Winter, T. (2007) Landscapes in the living memory. In N. Moore and Y. Whelan (eds) *Heritage, Memory and the Politics of Identity: New Perspectives on the Cultural Landscape* (pp. 133–148). Aldershot: Ashgate.
Wolff, J. (2012) After cultural theory: The power of images, the lure of immediacy. *Journal of Visual Culture* 11 (1), 3–19.
Wylie, J. (2007) *Landscape*. Abingdon: Routledge.
Yüksel, A. and Akgül, O. (2007) Postcards as affective image makers: An idle agent in destination marketing. *Tourism Management* 28 (3), 714–725.
Zembylas, M. (2006) Witnessing in the classroom: The ethics and politics of affect. *Educational Theory* 56 (3), 305–324.

Index

Acropolis, 72
advertising, 56–57
aesthetics
   manifestation in heritage tourist site design, 71–73
   of the picturesque, 40–41, 58, 109
   processes of aestheticization, 47
   of the sublime, 48, 92, 109
affect, 4, 25–28
   affective contagion, 76–77
   affective order of visuality, 92, 95–96
   affective registers, 72–73, 87
   and the body, 7, 81
   and cultural/social expression, 29
   definition, 25
   and intensity, 108
   manifestation in heritage tourist site design, 71–72
   neglect by semioticians, 75
   as precognitive, 80
   as process and product, 83
   and semiotic landscapes, 3
agencies of display, 35
Alhambra, 34, 48
Angkor Wat, 79, 85
archaeology, 3, 115–116, 118
Athens, 43, 72
attraction
   and affect, 109
   and the body, 72
   and product development, 57–58
Auschwitz-Birkenau, 78, 83
Australia
   ANZAC Day, 83
   Australian War Memorial, 69, 71
   role of Aboriginal culture in tourism, 24
   Uluru, 18, 28
authenticity
   construction of in tourism, 46
   and iconic images, 101
   and sight sacralization, 34
   and temporal depth, 103–105
Authorized Heritage Discourse, 8, 33, 38, 63, 103, 118, 120

Barthes, Roland, 19, 41, 48, 53
battlefields, 78, 100
Bile Beans sign, 112–113, 112, 115
body, the
   and affect, 27–28, 75–77
   as break with post-structuralism, 80
   experience of touristic sites, 4–5
   and the gaze, 24
   as instrument of research, 123
   as mediator of social memory, 81–85
   as photographer, 13, 30, 86–89
   physical engagement with heritage sites, 68–73
   and representation, 7
Bonnie and Clyde site, 46
brochures
   as authorized representations, 88
   and iconic images, 38
   and intensity, 109
   as markers, 19
   as marketing narratives, 56
   and memory, 78–79
   and the 'Other,' 21

brochures (*Continued*)
    as signifiers, 16
    and tourism studies, 4, 35
    and visuality, 3, 13

Cambodia, 79, 85
castles
    Bamburgh Castle, 88, 90–93, 90
    Bolton Castle, 110
    Castle Howard, 42
    Dustanburgh Castle, 70
    and intensity, 109–111
    Kritinia Castle, 44
    in UK heritage tourism, 40, 55
    Warkworth Castle, 55
    Windsor Castle, 40
colonialism, 6, 28
constructivism, 15
Cordoba, 88, 93–96, 102
crowds, 71–72, 82–83

Deleuze and Guattari, 25, 80
Derry, Ireland, 1
design of heritage tourist sites
    and agencies of display, 35
    embodied aspects, 68–73
    as representational practice, 54
destination image, 101, 105
discourse
    of heritage, ideological, 121
    vs. narrative, 54, 62
    in post-structuralist theory, 22
    of tourists, 24
dissonance, 84, 103

Eden Camp Modern History Theme
    Museum, 69
emotion
    and embodied memory, 81
    emergent theory on, 4
    evoked by sites of trauma, 2
    and intensity, 108
    manifestation in heritage tourist site
        design, 71–72, 75
    and semiotic landscapes, 3
    and visuality, 51
ethnomimesis, 41
everyday experience
    and affect, 99–100, 103

vs. the exotic, 106–107
and intensity, 112–114
exoticisation
    de-exoticisation, 10
    vs. the everyday, 104–105
    and the 'Other,' 21
    as purpose of tourism, 106
experience economies, 53–54, 60, 69–71

Flickr, 46, 88–96
Foucault, Michel, 20–21, 23, 54

genealogies of heritage, 37–45
    definition, 37
    in Greece, 43–45
    and intensity, 110–113
    and memory, 102
    in UK, 40–43
gift shops, 47, 60, 101
Gilpin, William, 39–40
Giralda Tower, 47, 48
Giza pyramids, Egypt, 33
Greece, 43–45, 72
guidebooks
    as authorized representations, 88
    in Greek heritage tourism, 43
    and intensity, 109
    as marketing narratives, 56
    and temporal depth, 104
    and tourism studies, 35

Hadrian's Wall, 40
hegemony, 36
Hollywood sign, 6–7, 7

icons, 18, 91, 101
ideology, 4, 22, 24, 121
immersive order of visuality, 93, 96
Indigenous culture, 24, 28, 37
intensity, 10, 99, 107–115, 119
intertextuality, 62–63

Jorvik Viking Centre, 69

Lévi-Strauss, Claude, 18

MacCannell, Dean, 4, 8, 11, 12, 19, 33, 46–47, 86

maps, 13, 19
marketing, 53–74
  and agencies of display, 35
  and authorized discourses, 9
  and embodied experience, 69–71
  local distinctiveness, 101–103
  organization of narratives, 63–68
  as performance, 62
  and Saussure, 19
  symbolic imagery in, 47
memory, 75–97
Mezquita, 93–96, 102
more-than-representational theory, 3, 25–31
  embodiment in heritage tourism, 70–71
  and photography, 5, 14
  in semiotic landscapes, 33, 117–119
  and visuality, 51
museums, 34, 66, 79, 118
myth, 41, 100

narrative, 49, 54–57, 63
national identity
  formation through heritage, 39, 41, 61, 64–65, 84, 121
  and power in heritage sites, 79
  role in shaping tourism, 8–9
  in semiotic landscapes of heritage tourism, 35, 118
  and tourist photography, 88
national monuments
  affective dimensions, 100
  Alhambra, 34
  Ancient Monuments Consolidation and Amendment Act of 1913 (UK), 47
  Ancient Monuments Protection Act of 1882 (UK), 40
  markers of monumentality, 46–47
  political meanings of, 79
national parks, 66
non-representational theory (NRT), 3, 4, 12, 14, 25–27
Northumberland hill forts, 66

Orientalism, 94–95
othering, 21, 24, 48

Peirce, Charles Sanders, 8, 12, 15, 18
performativity
  and embodied memory, 81
  emergent theory on, 4
  and engagement *in situ*, 9
  and exoticisation, 106–107
  and intensity, 111
  in marketing, 57, 62
  performative dynamism and heritage, 85
  'performative turn' in semiotics, 3, 68–69, 106, 119
  and tourist photography, 86–89
photography
  and affective contagion, 77, 85–97
  and authorized representations, 85–86
  and framing, 5
  and iconic images, 90–93
  importance of, 13
  as means to study affect, 29–31
  and memory, 87, 89, 96
  as performance, 30, 86–89, 94, 122
  in semiotic theory, 14
  and tourism studies, 4
  and visuality, 2
politics
  in more-than-representational accounts, 51
  and (non-)representation, 14
  political economy of heritage tourism, 120–21
  semiotic reductionism of, 67–68
postcards
  as authorized representations, 88
  at Ground Zero site, 72
  and iconic images, 38, 90–93, 101
  as markers, 19
  as marketing narratives, 56
  and memory, 78–79
  and the 'Other,' 21
  as signifiers, 16
  and tourism studies, 4, 35
  and tourist photography, 88, 90–93
post-structuralism
  deconstruction of semiotic landscapes as texts, 79
  examples of, 25
  and photography, 14

post-structuralism (*Continued*)
  theorists of, 8
  and tourism studies, 12, 20–24, 123
  and visuality, 3
power
  and authorized discourses, 103
  and (non-)representation, 14
  in post-structuralist theory, 20–23, 79
  in semiotic landscapes of heritage tourism, 35, 118
  and Uluru tourism, 28
Puente Romano, 93–94

reflective order of visuality, 91
Remembrance Sunday, 78, 83
representation
  critiques of, 26–27
  limits of, 12
  as performance, 89
  role in emerging more-than-representational approaches, 117–19
  of subaltern in historical memory, 79
  violence of, 24
  and visuality, 3
Rhodes, Greece, 43, 44, 65
Robben Island, 78
Roman ruins
  in Spanish heritage tourism, 93–94
  in UK heritage tourism, 39–40, 47, 66, 115
ruins
  and 19th-century tourism, 6
  and intensity, 109–111
  Roman, 39–40, 47, 66, 93–94, 115
  in UK heritage tourism, 58
rural-historic, 61, 64

Saussure, Ferdinand de, 8, 12, 15, 58
Scotland, 51, 58, 67
semiotic landscapes, 8, 13, 33, 58–60
sight sacralization, 34, 37, 46
signifiers
  in Peirce, 17–18
  in post-structuralist theory, 20
  in Saussure, 16–17
  sensory, 69–71
  the 'typical,' 101
signs
  vs. experiences, 118–119

heritage as sign of itself, 48–49
  in structural theory, 16–17
social media, 46, 57, 88–96. *see also* Flickr
Spain
  Alhambra, 34, 48
  Cordoba, 88, 93–96, 102
  Giralda Tower, 47, 48
Stonehenge, 39, 40
structuralism, 12, 14, 15–19, 25
Stukeley, William, 39
symbolic capital, 51
syntagmatic meaning, 58–59

technology, 67–68, 76–77
temporal depth, 99, 103–105
textuality, 3–4
Thrift, Nigel, 12, 26, 72–73, 80
tourism, 30
  as employer, 113–114
  as field of study, 3
  as industry, 53–55
  as marketable product, 53–74
  as performance, 30, 62, 105–107, 111
  and photography, 30, 122
  and representation, 119
  tourist gaze, 2, 23
  and visuality, 2
tourism area life cycle, 105
Tower of London, 40
Turkey, 43–44

Uluru, 18, 28
UNESCO World Heritage Sites, 94
United Kingdom. *see also* ruins
  English country houses, 36, 42, 58–59, 59
  English Heritage, 42, 47, 58, 66
  formation of Englishness, 41, 61
  heritage tourism industry in, 21–23, 38–41, 47, 58–60, 61, 64
  leisurization of heritage in, 61
  National Trust, 40, 42, 47
  prehistory, 39, 40, 65–67
  representation of historical periods, 65–67
  Scotland, 51, 58
  Stonehenge, 39
  Wales, 58

York, 112–113
Yorkshire, 50, 67, 77, 81, 87, 110
Urry, John, 4, 8, 11, 12, 15, 23, 45, 57, 69
USS Arizona memorial, 16

visitor centres, 47
visuality
  affective order, 92
  dominance of, 2, 13
  of heritage attractions, 37, 38, 43, 45–50, 49, 58
  immersive order, 93
  in MacCannell, 86
  of 'national' stories, 65
  reflective order, 91

Wales, 58
Washington Zoo, 46
Whitby Abbey, 40
Wilberforce, William, 67
World Trade Center/Ground Zero site, 72, 78

For Product Safety Concerns and Information please contact our EU Authorised Representative:

Easy Access System Europe

Mustamäe tee 50

10621 Tallinn

Estonia

gpsr.requests@easproject.com

www.ingramcontent.com/pod-product-compliance
Ingram Content Group UK Ltd.
Pitfield, Milton Keynes, MK11 3LW, UK
UKHW022217250326

4937IPUK00005B/27